Out of Grace

An unlikely journey through
Guatemala's haunted highlands

Cynthia Renwick

ISBN:1499790031
ISBN-13:9781499790030

This book is for Paul Brace, who I never knew but will always remember; and for Lisa Jury, who was so wise and brave in the face of tragedy

It's gonna rain ... and thunder ... and lightning.
How frightening!
Oh me ... oh my ... I think I'm gonna die.

-Outward Bound camp
song

PROLOGUE

Here is how I always start this story when I tell it: "When I lived in Guatemala, I was struck by lightning on a volcano with a group of tourists, and a guy in our group died."

This tragic event occupied a period of less than 3 seconds, but it was one of the most significant moments in my journey, and in the lives of all who were there with me on Pacaya that day. I usually start this way because it is the thing that gets people's attention. In truth, I did not really know him, but telling the story is a way for me to explain. It is a doorway to excavating the fear, the helplessness, and the truth that Guatemala showed me.

I left for a year of anthropological study in Guatemala in January 2002, four months after the September 11th attacks. Traveling at that time was ridiculous, as you may remember, with four-hour lines, beefed-up security, and constant announcements over the intercom that we were at "threat level orange." Without the media storm following 9/11, or the paranoia that gripped the American population and the government's defense and security systems, I could have had a much different experience in Central America. However, because I traveled when I did, my Guatemalan journey began with terror.

1

My Fulbright lasted 10 months, and over the following five years, I returned to Guatemala every winter, from December through April or May, between contract archaeology jobs. I went there to write about coming of age in a post-9/11 world, to find answers to universal questions, to seek peace and truth, to find a sense of closure for Paul's death, and mostly to find a way to understand, explain, and overcome the fear and loneliness I carried.

When I'm telling the story, and they hear about Paul being struck by lightning on the volcano, most people appear fascinated or stunned, or they say something like "really?" or "wow!" or "did you get struck by lightning, too?"

If I can, I explain everything. I tell about the sense of helplessness after the rescue and learning Paul was dead. I tell about the Methodist faith I grew up with, and how I lost it early in my journey. I tell about the loneliness of not having God to turn to, one day after the next, and about the crime, the fear, and the people who told me I should carry a gun. I tell about the Tz'utujiil Maya, and how they live terror, and loss, and darkness everyday in the midst of the jaw-dropping beauty of Lake Atitlan. I tell about the drugs, and the search for spirituality, and how San Pedro la Laguna was like a magnet for people who were lost, like me.

As I tell it, I remember the vivid colors; the rancid, sweet, and earthy smells; the wrinkled faces; and mornings by the lakeshore with volcanoes on the horizon, and wood smoke, and cups of coffee, and hangovers. I remember how Guatemala and the Pacaya Volcano haunted me for so long, and the way the Mayan people and the land I grew to love are so haunted by the past.

I wrote this book in San Pedro, at my parents' house in Baltimore, and in hotel rooms throughout the U.S. as I traveled for archaeology work. The events, characters, dates, and experiences in these pages are all very real and the dialogue has been recreated as faithfully as possible from my journals, notes, and memory. Names have been changed as requested and to protect the innocent.

This is the story, from the beginning, of a personal connection between religion and fear, of a country's fall from grace, and of a young woman on a bittersweet journey away from God, through a war-torn and haunted land.

GUATEMALA CITY

Guatemala is a land of contradiction. There are marimba bands playing on street corners while political prisoners are tortured in dungeons underground. The elite bare their light-skinned legs, and dance salsa in the Zona Viva, while the Mayan elders in the countryside shiver and scream out from nightmares—bloody memories of *la violencia*. Politicians fly around in helicopters drinking martinis and organizing assassinations, while emaciated children help their families pull shacks back together after a mudslide destroys a village. It is a place where the very rich and very poor live side by side. The volcanic skyline speaks of the land's vast beauty. The squalid ruins of the Mayan civilization portray its wretchedness. The air is often filled at once with the great sweetness of flowers and the putrid stench of filth and decay.

I begin my journey in the sprawling capital, Guatemala City (or Guate as it is known by the locals), and step from the terminal into the Guatemalan air trembling with excitement. The blazing heat is a welcome shock after leaving Baltimore in January but so dry that I become thirsty immediately. As the taxi lurches from the airport towards my hotel, the city that appears around me is not

4

what I expected. I breathe in deeply, trying to capture a magical scent from the enchanted land I have anticipated and prepared for, but am revolted by odors of trash, rotten vegetables, urine and feces, and black clouds of diesel. I look for the colonial Latin architecture I read about in my anthropology class, but see shanties and houses made of cardboard and scraps of corrugated tin. They are heaped on top of mounds of garbage, and stacked into narrow ravines.

As we enter the central Zone 1, the concrete buildings are cracked and falling down from regular earthquakes, and rebar sticks out haphazardly in every direction. This part of the city looks like a war zone with political graffiti on every wall and piles of rubble spilling into the streets. Windows are covered with iron bars or metal gates to keep out the thieves.

The Hotel Cristal has an armed guard who answers the door. Across the street, there is a Mayan woman hunched around two filthy children. They watch me pay the taxi driver and go inside.

My first observation in Guate the next day is the sheer number of flies. I fan them away from my eggs and coffee, and shake their dead carcasses from my shoes. Visiting the market near my hotel, I find apocalyptic hoards of them buzzing through the stalls, landing on all the fruit, chicken, leather, and textiles, and swarming around people's callused feet and wrinkled faces. Mayan women, wrapped in layers of cloth, fan them away constantly while selling tortillas. They encrust the eyes of stray dogs with sagging nipples, that are dodging kicks, picking through trash, and sleeping in the gutters.

My second observation is that in every storefront, on every corner, and behind every locked door, are men with big guns, dark uniforms, and bent fingers resting on triggers.

Though I know from my research that Guatemala

City isn't exactly a vacation destination, I am dismayed by the heat, noise, and grime. I suppose it seems unromantic. On the streets, filthy buses spew clouds of diesel smoke and roar down the street so loudly that I have to cover my ears. But I try to ignore it and keep going, setting up appointments, planning my research, and learning the city's history by touring museums and the National Palace.

After a few days, I learn to navigate the city and it becomes more familiar. I figure out the major bus routes, and to negotiate for the local price - 1 Quetzal (about 12 cents at the time). Before very long, I am able to ignore the trash on the floor, and the smell of urine, and the other passengers, who squish in beside me and stare because they don't know what to make of a white girl riding the bus through one of the few Central American cities that doesn't see many tourists.

As I travel around the capital, making living arrangements and meeting with my contacts at the Museum of Indigenous Clothing and the University, the reality of this city's condition sets in. Every day in the newspaper, which I read to improve my Spanish, there are reports of kidnappings, murders, fatal bus crashes, rape. I start looking over my shoulder all the time to see who is following me because with white skin, red hair, and freckles, I am sure I stand out. Every evening, as the sun sinks, I scramble to get back to my hotel before dark, because I have been told that it isn't safe to be out at night.

And there is real evidence that Guate becomes a battleground between dusk and dawn. Graffiti appears overnight on the walls. *Gringo Go Home. Burn Yankee Burn. Murder. Assesino.* I have to wear earplugs to drown out the sounds of breaking glass and shouting, and now find myself thankful for the armed guard. When it is finally safe to emerge in the morning, store owners are washing the sidewalks to get rid of the shit and vomit, and the lingering smell of urine.

A few weeks into January, I rent an apartment in the safest area I can find, and enroll in anthropology classes at the nearby University of the Valley of Guatemala (UVG). My Fulbright is a financial scholarship to cover nearly a year in the country, and my project involves studying at UVG for a semester, dedicated to learning the country's history, studying Mayan anthropology and archaeology, perfecting my Spanish, and privately learning all I can about textiles. I plan to spend the last five months of my grant period *in the field*. To me, this is the most exciting and authentic part, and what will finally make me an ethnographer, a true anthropologist. According to my original Fulbright proposal, I will study textiles in two small villages in Alta Verapáz—an impoverished indigenous area, particularly scarred by the massacres of the 1980s. I plan to examine how the changing styles and designs of their clothing tell this dark story.

I live in Zone 15, the sprawling suburban area of the capitol with a maze of sterile, cookie-cutter "*colonias*" radiating off of a tree-lined boulevard with grass planted in the median. It has wide lanes and stoplights, strip malls and drive-thrus. In this part of town, people have dogs as pets, fill Viagra prescriptions at the pharmacy, go to work in Mazdas, and buy Pop Tarts, Chinese clothes, and cosmetics at the "Hiper Paiz" (a Walmart-like superstore). They rent new releases from Blockbuster, and buy their kids Happy Meals from McDonald's on their birthday. In so many ways it is just like home. Strangely, it is this similarity and this portrait of globalization that makes living in Guatemala City so foreign.

After a few weeks, I am surprised again when homesickness starts to kick in. There are few international students at the University, and I miss speaking English. I miss friendship. Everyone at UVG is cold-shouldered and distant, and I desperately long for the kind, glowing, happy side of Central America I hoped to find. To put it mildly, Guatemala City is not what I wanted it to be. Even in

Zone 15, there are twelve-foot walls around each home, with broken glass shards jutting out of the top, ready to slice open the hand of anyone crazy enough to intrude. The walls are one of many symbols of the fear that permeates the air, lingering like a ghost over the entire city. People walking down the street keep hollow, fixed gazes, never smiling, never making contact, or recognizing a human face. The whole population seems to stare into the middle distance, except the few who sink their eyes into my flesh, their gaze piercing with malice. Instinctually, I find myself clenching my hand around the pepper spray in my pocket, ready for anything.

Even in this neighborhood I hear gunshots ring out at night. People walking down the street scream at each other and have fist fights, guard dogs bark and growl, and car tires squeal. It is impossible to ignore the country's history of real terror—terror that seems to come to life when the sun goes down. It is a new brand of evil for me—one that doesn't just haunt people's sleepless nights, but actually comes into their houses and kills them.

Once I have the apartment, I spend my evenings sitting on the balcony, gazing off at the sunset behind the volcanoes, thinking too much, and strangely missing home. I never expect to be homesick, but it comes anyway. My whole life, I have wanted to leave—to travel and live in the world beyond the U.S. But with each day that passes in Guate with no one to share it with, the loneliness grows. And as hard as I try to forget and to live in the moment, all I can think about is my ex-boyfriend back home, and how terrified I am of him finding someone else before we have a chance to "try again."

During that first month, I deal with my discomfort by praying a lot. I wander in and out of churches throughout the city and kneel in front of altars and light candles like the other women. I remember the jolly and faithful side of Central America I know from my yearly church trips to Costa Rica. There, we work with an organization called

Volunteer in Missions (VIM) to teach vacation bible school and complete needed construction projects. At that rural Methodist retreat center outside of Ciudad Quesada, magical things happened to my Christian faith every year. I stood in prayer circles 50 people wide, and clasped hands surging with energy. I clenched my eyes shut and let tears roll down my cheeks for joy and the love I felt for everyone, and for Jesus, my comfort, my shelter. And I sang, and sang, and sang—all the songs so full of love and joy and peace. Singing was my favorite thing about religion, because believing in god and feeling the spirit were the perfect excuses to belt it out, whenever I felt moved. At school or at home when I tried to sing, people just rolled their eyes and told me to shut up. But the VIM people loved it, claiming that the louder a person sang, the better. They frequently broke into song spontaneously, singing "Halleluiah!" or "I will Praise Him" or "Our God is an Awesome God!" and rousing an entire crowd to sing along. Year after year, we spent that week in February conducting ourselves like southern Baptists at a revival.

But in Guatemala City, the sky is filled with shouting instead of song, and the thick haze of smog chokes my lungs. Where I expect to find toucans and palm trees and *pura vida*, there are shacks and bandits and desperation. Where I expect to feel lush, moist tropical breezes and forested views, the smog is suffocating and the hillsides are dead. Everything is dry. Brown. Brittle. Burning. In Costa Rica, everyone was clean and happy and fed. But here, people smell of sewage and poverty, and the smiles on their faces do not quite hide their deeper grief. For the loss of their heritage. For their brothers and sisters and children who died in the war. For their basic human rights.

And I don't expect to feel so many eyes on me, penetrating me with their gaze, trying to see inside of me, hating me for my money and my white skin. I always feel them watching—while I buy tickets for movies with money that could feed their starving children, and while I sit eating too much food in restaurants above the street. Day after day, I shove expensive American food down my throat to feel more at home, while people lurk around me, starving. Barefoot. Asking for change. Asking if I want to buy a *chalina* or a *bolsita,* or a pen embroidered with my name.

When men hiss and beckon to me, I feel unclean under their stares. I imagine them, cornering me in some alley, with crooked, gaping, and gold teeth, dirty fingernails clutching my arms and holding me down. Sometimes, when I don't quite make it home before dark, I become so terrified that I can almost smell the liquor on their breath and feel the warm wet rasp of it on my face as they attack me. For the most part, they never come too close, like they know I will fight, but still they yell at me from across crowded streets, saying "Ey! Where you going?" They hiss at me the same way they hiss at dogs. It is like they are hunting me, just waiting for the moment I let my guard down.

In February, I get a call from the embassy, requesting that I come in for a security briefing, and to get photographed for my Fulbright ID badge. At the gate, they send me through a metal detector and take away my passport. I show them my pepper spray, and ask if I need to leave it behind, and they shrug and wave me through.

Walking inside the embassy is like being transported to an alternate reality. The sound of clicking heels bounces off the linoleum, air conditioning blasts down from the ceiling ducts, and the smell of coffee wafts up from a café in the basement. A blonde military guard with a crew cut leads me to the conference room where stacks of lists and carbon copies sit in front of everyone, and a man with a sticker that says "Hello! My name is … Patrick," stands at the end of the table, droning in monotone.

"Number four," Patrick reads from one of the packets. "Don't hail a taxi on the street. There have been a number of reported kidnappings from unregistered taxi services. Number five: don't ride the intercity and rural buses. Bus travel in Guatemala is very dangerous and even first-class buses are attacked on major routes. If you must ride a bus, do it with extreme caution, and only during the day, never at night. And don't put your bags on the roof. They will be stolen."

My Fulbright contact at the US embassy told me over the phone that this security briefing was mandatory, and would be "like an orientation to Guatemala." And as Patrick slides me a packet without interrupting his monotone, I realize that I am not in college anymore, and orientations given by men with manicured nails, shiny black shoes, and badges clipped to their silk ties have nothing to do with ice-breakers, name games, or getting to know each other.

I am so curious about the others, sitting attentively around the table and making love to their packets. I want to know if any of them are Fulbright scholars like me, anthropologists, or potential friends. But none of them look like students or anthropologists or even travelers. These are business people. One man across from me with a Rolex and slicked-back hair scribbles notes on a legal pad. A woman at the end of the table, wearing a white linen dress and a straw hat, has her face scrunched up with concentration, nodding steadily to every word Patrick says.

"Here in the capitol, American tourists have been robbed, raped, and murdered in broad daylight," he continues. "If you're based here, don't live in Zone 1, or Zone 4, or Zone 5. There's a list of approved zones on page 3. If you hike in any of the national parks be sure to hire an armed guide. Bandits have made a habit of robbing and raping tourists. There are also still some lingering guerilla groups in the countryside, so you can't just go wandering around out there without protection. Don't carry around huge amounts of money, and don't go outside after dark, under any circumstances."

My eyes glaze over and I flip the pages of the packet without looking at them and shiver from the air conditioning. Before I left for Guatemala, everyone was full of advice and warnings, and it was starting to sound like a broken record. Don't drink the water. Don't carry a purse. Don't go out at night. Don't. Don't. Don't. Don't. People sent me newspaper articles from all over the world, on tourists who went missing, or got into trouble over drugs, or got killed, and suggested certain books I might read about the violence of the 80s and the oppression of dictatorial governments. "Maybe you should carry a gun," they said.

"Never go outside after dark," Patrick says again from the front of the room, his monotone dripping with boredom. He looks up. "All you have to do is read the newspaper to understand why."

After one month, I understand and I don't need to listen to this. Some of my classes at UVG end after dark, and coming home involves hyper-tuning my senses, constantly looking over my shoulder, and instructing the taxi driver on exactly where to go so he won't take me for a ride. I am always grateful for the good Spanish I learned as a child from my adopted El Salvadoran brother and sister. I have a good accent, and I can communicate myself well. It earns me respect in vulnerable moments. When toothless, foul-smelling men come too close and try to touch me, I spit out things in Spanish like, *go away, asshole. Leave me alone, carajo. Vete a tomar por culo.* They often reel back in shock, bow their heads and apologize quietly, saying, *"disculpa señora.* I'm sorry." My Spanish is my ace in the hole. It is there like a weapon, every time I need it.

Patrick hands out more papers—triplicates—with white, pink and yellow carbon copies. "You will need to register your address with personnel, and if you travel, you must file a trip itinerary." He waves the triplicates in the air. "File these with the embassy *two weeks* prior to your departure from Guatemala City." He stops and sips from a bottle of water. The label says *agua pura Salvavidas*. Translated literally: Pure, life-saving water.

A plastic-looking woman with heels and a blond perm comes into the room and sets my ID badge down in front of me, her acrylic nails clicking against the table. Patrick drones on. "In your packet, you will find the Department of State information sheet. Please direct your attention to the 'crime' section at the bottom of page two." I flip the page and glance down.

He reads to us aloud: "The number of violent crimes reported by U.S. citizens and other foreigners has increased in recent years. Incidents include, but are not limited to, assault, theft, armed robbery, carjacking, rape, kidnapping, and murder. Criminals usually operate in groups of four or more and are considerably confrontational and violent."

I examine the badge. It is still warm from the laminator and I have an urge to press it to my face. There is a photo of me on one side, with the U.S. embassy seal, my birthday, my classification as a Fulbright scholar and as a "temporary official." On the back is a list of phone numbers for 24-hour emergency response, military police, and hospitals. I clip the badge to a metal chain and hang it around my neck, feeling suddenly important and worldly.

"Gang members are often well-armed with sophisticated weaponry and they sometimes use massive amounts of force ... widespread narcotics and alien smuggling activities can make remote areas especially dangerous...."

I am not listening anymore. I think about my fieldwork. Now that I have a badge, I feel like a real anthropologist. I have all the materials—a bin filled with notebooks and zip lock bags and sharpies and film. I have three cameras, a digital recorder, crayons and paper to give the children, an 18-month extension on my visa, and a badge that makes me a U.S. government official. I have no idea what I will find "in the field." I only know that I want it to be big and sacred and magical. I want to meet a shaman, to learn herbal remedies and stories of spirits and ancestors. To make friends with an old Mayan woman who will teach me to make tortillas, how to weave on a backstrap loom and dye the threads with indigo—one who will call me "*m'ija*" or "*mi niña*" and be like the wise grandmother I never had. More than anything I want the Mayan people to teach me, to show me from their ancient wisdom how to be closer to nature, and more in harmony with the earth. I want to talk to red-tailed hawks, like a Cherokee Indian. I want to crush herbs and flowers and cure illnesses, and ride horses bareback with my hair whipping out behind me in the wind.

"Though there is no evidence that Americans are particularly targeted," Patrick continues, "criminals look for every opportunity to attack, so all travelers should remain constantly vigilant. Stay in the main tourist destinations. Do not explore back roads or isolated paths near tourist sites. Pay close attention to your surroundings, especially when walking or when driving in Guatemala City. Refrain from displaying expensive-looking jewelry, large amounts of money, or other valuable items. Finally, if confronted by criminals, resistance may provoke a more violent response."

He shuffles the papers against the table, smoothing the edges and lining them up. "That's it," he says, folding everything into a shiny, leather briefcase. "Are there any questions?"

CHICKEN BUS

I travel out of Guatemala City for the first time on a Friday, three weeks after the security briefing, without filling out my carbon copy forms and turning them in to the embassy. I don't care about their two-weeks notice and it doesn't seem like they care much either, or if they even know I exist at all. I have heard nothing from anyone since the orientation, and don't expect to. I figure—how will they know I'm not in town? They can't.

The Fulbright, I have started to learn, is not like being in the Peace Corps, or doing semesters abroad in college, with paid training, and advisors, and other international students to be my friends. In Guate, there is no one watching over me. No one making sure I am settled in, or up and running on my project. The Fulbright is an *independent* research project, for college graduates who are supposed to be educated and grown up.

But I hate the city so much that most days I try as hard as possible to make it feel like I am not in Guatemala at all. My classes at the University have turned out to be little more than an opportunity to practice my Spanish comprehension, and I haven't made any friends. And hiding in my apartment after dark, eating Hot Pockets and bowls of Kraft Macaroni and Cheese in front of the cable

TV is nothing like anthropology.

Then one Saturday I find the intercity bus terminal in Zone 4, a squalid market area of Guatemala City where the air smells putrid with rot, and both dogs and people are crusted in sores. I hoist myself through the back door of a multi-colored bus and work my way down the very crowded aisle. In fact they are often called "chicken" buses by tourists because of how packed in the people are. That and they are often seen loaded with livestock. Before I have a chance to find a seat or take in the earthy quality of the other highland-bound passengers, shouting erupts in the street. A man with a face mask runs past our bus, smashing a lead pipe against the windows. The glass shatters onto the passengers.

There are a few quiet cries of surprise.

Our bus lurches casually away, with some passengers still climbing on and squeezing past each other, some brushing glass shards off of their jackets, and others staring emotionlessly and glassy-eyed into the street.

We are bound for the Mayan areas near Lake Atitlán, and many people on the bus are wearing *traje*, the indigenous dress. The women are comfortable in their traditional woven *huipiles* and the men look natural in their straw hats. These vibrant colors worn by the Maya Indians who inhabit the department of Sololá are part of the reason the caldera of Atitlán is often called one of the most beautiful lakes in the world. It is a growing tourist center, where in addition to cheap textiles, there are also adobe houses with tiles roofs; cobbled streets; three towering volcanoes; crisp, cold water for swimming; and a deep sense of mystery and tragic history.

As soon as we pull away from Zone 4, I realize how much I have been suffocating from the smog and paranoia and dry air. This is the first time I have worked up enough courage to ignore the embassy's advice, and I think I am ready at last for the cultural adventure this bus journey promises.

The bus inches through the streets towards the highway without ever fully stopping, and people run along side and leap on, and a young boy swings out the door and climbs up on the roof to stow the passengers' burlap sacks and baskets. Silver stickers across the back window glitter in the sun and read, "*Diós bendiga este bús.*" God bless this bus. A beaded purple rosary hangs from the rearview mirror. Another sign above the driver's head says, "Jesus is my copilot."

We weave up into the mountains, away from Chimaltenango, and out of the sprawling haze of the capital. I sit back against my seat and for the first time since arriving in Guatemala I begin to breathe deeply again. The air in the highlands is so much cleaner and clear enough to see the sky. Looking east from the Pan American Highway I can see forever—rugged, rolling hills, terraced with crops. To the west I see blue sky, steep rocky slopes, and a landscape dotted with volcanoes. Around every bend in the road, there is another triangle in the sky.

There are 33 volcanoes in Guatemala. The entire western half of the country is one long string of them, one after the next, from Mexico all the way down to El Salvador. The whole Highland area sits along a convergence between the Cocos Plate and the Caribbean Plate, where over the past 5 million years, a volcanic chain has formed bordering the Pacific, stretching from Guatemala to Panama. There are 68 volcanoes in the entire chain. In Guatemala, four are active. Volcanic eruptions and major earthquakes are a fact of life.

Though the volcanoes are relatively young in geological terms, they are one of the only things that have remained constant for the people who have lived here over the millennia. Everything else has changed so fast that if the Mayan kings were still alive today, it would hardly be recognizable as the same land. The Maya have lived in this region of Guatemala for over 3,000 years, but today the Guatemala with high rise buildings in the capital, intercity buses pouring black clouds of diesel smoke into the atmosphere, and white tourists with flip flops and huge backpacks stuffed with things they think they need, would seem a totally foreign place.

Once, in this exact area, huge ceremonial centers were the hubs of activity—pyramids, temples, and cities, with trade routes, and days when everyone converged to celebrate in religious ceremonies. Jaguars and spider monkeys roamed the hills. Scarlet macaws and resplendent quetzals perched on branches of Ceiba trees, with their long tail plumes hanging down, and orchids grew on the branches. The area that is now Guatemala City would have been Kaminaljuyu, a Mayan mound city that flourished in the middle Formative period and is as impressive to archaeologists as the temples at Palenque and Tikal. Today, the site has been swallowed by urban development, but archaeologists have found obsidian blades, jade beads, metates, and Las Charcas pottery. Only a small green patch with two mounds and a few interpretive signs remains. The wildlife and the forests of ancient Guatemala are also gone—decimated over the years to make way for crops, mined for natural resources, destroyed by plagues, and replaced by dirty cities full of concrete and smog.

By the time Pedro de Alvarado and his army arrived in 1523, the Mayan civilization was already in decline, ravaged by intertribal warfare. The ensuing Spanish conquest was traumatic and brutal, not just because of the power of European weapons and the speed of their horses, or diseases like smallpox, influenza, and measles which reduced the population by 90 percent, but also because of the forced spread of Christianity. With the establishment of a Creole government, the building of missions, and the enslavement of the indigenous population to work on *fincas*, the doctrine of Catholic fear quickly swept over the land.

Today, there are more living Mayan people here in the Highlands than anywhere else in Central America, speaking 23 different indigenous languages. Since the conquest, Spanish and Mayan blood have mixed together, creating a race called *ladinos,* and giving birth to a fierce brand of racism. Today almost everyone in Guatemala has a mixture of Spanish and Mayan blood to some degree. The darker skin or more Mayan blood a person has, the lower his class. The lighter a person's skin, the more Spanish blood he has, and the more elite he is. Pure-blood Spanish Creoles born in Guatemala are the power-holders. Pure-blood Mayans are the field laborers and prostitutes, and often work like slaves.

I gaze at the passing landscape and see people walking along the roadsides bundled up in brilliant layers of textiles. The women carry heaping baskets of ripe fruit and squawking chickens and burlap sacks as big as cows on their heads; the men have hoes and machetes for work in the field, and immense bundles of firewood hanging down over their backs.

Looking off over the ridge to the east, I imagine Pedro de Alvarado and his armies, struggling up these steep hillsides, weighted down by guns and armor, and with crucifixes and rosaries jangling as they approach. I imagine the priests, in black robes leading the procession, carrying bibles, tripping over rocks and panting from the climb. I imagine slaves that they have captured from the east, people who have agreed to convert and to learn Spanish, carrying heavy loads, prodded on by the barrels of guns stuck in their backs, by the threat of death.

The Guatemala the conquistadors found would have been a much quieter place back then, without the roar of generators and buses. There would have been no cantinas with loud Spanish pop music blaring, or people stumbling out into the street and passing out face down, half off the sidewalk, where everyone just ignores them, steps over them, and does not even stop to think "what a shame." The air would not have been full of the constant pounding of hammers, the streets would not have been full of trash, the walls of every building would not be etched with words like *busca Diós* (seek God), *Jesús es su única esperanza* (Jesus is your only hope), next to the words *huecos* (gays) and *asesino* (murder). Only parts of the landscape would have been the same, with those same rugged hills, terraced fields, red volcanic sunsets, and ridges cloaked in cold fog.

Just north of Tecpán and the Mayan ruins at Iximche, our bus pulls over and a man in a business suit gets on, carrying a case of small bottles. He moves up and down the aisle, passing them out, encouraging us to open them, and rub a little on our skin. The woman next to me unscrews the lid and smells inside, then dabs her finger in and smudges a glob of greasy white gel across her arm. Everyone else does the same, and a waxy eucalyptus smell fills the bus. Meanwhile, the salesman climbs back down the aisle (the bus has gotten quite crowded by this time) and wedges himself into a space at the front, turns to face us and holds up a bible in his left hand.

"Hello, my friends. If you will permit me a moment of your time, I would like to share a little bit of the word of God."

I look around and see a few nods of approval, then the turn of heads, cocked attentively, ready to listen. I half tune him out and turn back towards the window. I can't quite follow his Spanish, and only catch snippets of what he is saying, but I hear the word "*pecadores*" over and over again. Sinners … sinners … sinners.

Looking east over the Guatemalan countryside, his sermon fades into the background and I watch the dry, brown hills streak by, feeling the dryness of my mouth, wishing things were lush and tropical and green. I feel an uneasy twist in my gut—not just because of the way the bus is flying around curves, but because of something I have been sensing, but have yet been unable to grasp. Over the past month I have wandered around the presidential palace courtyards, visited conquest memorials and Catholic cathedrals, and taken anthropological notes at the Museo Ixchel and the Popol Vuh Museum in Guatemala City. Along the way, an inexplicable discomfort, and a sense of fear, helplessness, and loneliness has grown inside me, expanding exponentially with each thing I learn about the country's history. I thought it was just the chaos of Guate, but on this bus I am starting to see that it is something much bigger.

"And me?" the salesman at the front of the chicken bus says, clenching his eyes shut and bringing his fist to his chest. "I have given my life to Jesus Christ. God sent Him down to save us from sin, and through His love, we can find peace. Through His love, we can find eternal happiness. Through Him, we can be saved." He raises his right hand in the air and begins to pray. I can't help but feel like this is all quite ridiculous.

The woman beside me drops her head, holds her hands out with the palms up, and begins muttering, "*Si. Ay Diós. Porfavor. Cuidame. Cuida mis niños.*"

Many people are praying and moaning, and a chorus of whispers fills the bus. I watch the scene unfolding and feel like things are oddly distorted. Here I am, admiring these Mayan people for retaining their heritage—their traditional Mayan dress, agricultural methods, language—and they are worshiping a Christian God. It doesn't make any sense. It strikes me that these people only believe in God and Jesus the way they do, because of Pedro de Alvarado and the Catholic Church. Because of the conquest. Because they were threatened into believing it with guns.

And then, wasn't I threatened into believing it too? Wasn't I told over and over again by preachers and nuns that if I didn't believe in God, I would go to hell? Didn't I think that if I didn't pray in my bed at night, monsters would leap out of the closet, and someone would come into my house and take me away? Hurt me? If no one had ever scared me with stories of the Devil and sin and hell, would I believe in any God at all?

It happens in an instant. My belief is strong one minute and then it is gone the next. Vaporized. Like being struck by lightning. If I really think about the origins of Christianity, about the way it all began, with killing and oppression, and people in power forcing others to believe—then it becomes so obvious that I want to slap myself. In this moment, my logical mind says only this: *None of it actually exists.* These are stories told for political gain. No wonder most people are afraid to talk about their faith. If they really start questioning it, they will find the truth staring back at them, saying "duh...." Christianity is like a window we choose to see the world through, without ever noticing all the scratches on the glass.

The bus lurches around a corner and I feel a clenching in my stomach. I try to brush aside all the consequences of not believing. But what if I die now and there is no heaven? What is the point of any of it if life is just ... over? What if I stop believing, but it is real, and I get stranded at the Pearly Gates where Saint Peter won't let me in. I realize as I try to pray that there is no real protection in all this muttering. There is no Holy Spirit guiding me. I am alone. Terribly, bitterly alone.

I think about my choices: I can just keep on believing blindly, telling myself what I always have in the face of doubt, that all these reasons not to believe are just manifestations of the devil, trying to tempt me away. Or I can step away from my faith for a while and look at the world with my own eyes. Evaluate with a clean slate. The second option has the painful feel of truth to it but also fills me with quivering pangs of excitement. There is no time like the present. It means ending a lifelong relationship with God—with a being that suddenly seems not to exist at all—with a mode of thought that has saved me from suicide, from drugs, from a life of sin, from terror in the night. So what will save me now? It will be like getting a divorce from the faith, which has been everything to me. Everything about my life and sense of comfort will change.

Atheist. I try the word out in my mind, and I say it softly under my breath. It tastes funny, like dirt, and I want to chew it, but not spit it out.

The bus swings around a curve and nearly comes up on two wheels. I gasp and clutch the seat, staring down at the cliff that dropped off sharply below us. A surge of adrenaline pumps down my spine.

Out of habit, I close my eyes and try to ask for help, then I realize that if I am going to be an atheist, I can't exactly pray. With my eyes still closed, I do the only thing I can. I begin to focus on the sound of my breath, counting my inhales and exhales, shallow at first, then drawing them out, each one longer and longer. I visualize. I picture myself surviving Guatemala. I see the end, imagining myself walking down the terminal at BWI airport, with Mom and Dad at the end holding out their arms to me, welcoming me home. I imagine that this Fulbright nightmare is over. That I am home. Safe at last.

Without saying "Amen," I open my eyes, and the salesman has a bottle of cream open and is spreading it on the back of his hand.

"This cream," he says, "is Mayan medicine—a gift from God. It will heal you, and it will make you strong. If you have sunspots or cancers, it will take them away. If you have a cold, you can rub the cream on your throat and it will soothe you." He looks at me and winks. "It will even help you to lose weight."

By the time we get to Los Encuentros, the driving has become more than terrifying. The people nearby are crammed in so tightly that no one can really breathe. The idea that praying would make me a hypocrite becomes lodged in my mind, and I realize that I have no way to manage fear without faith.

I'd like to say that when I catch my first glimpse of Lake Atitlán, it is so beautiful that I hear angels singing and forget to be afraid of the swerving and lurching and cursing. I'd like to say that the sun is hanging over those volcanoes just right, and that the water is dazzling blue, and that the hillsides are rugged and green and glowing. I'd like to say that when we first come over that pass at Los Encuentros, I am spellbound, and I forget everything else, and an awed shiver runs up my spine. But by the time Atitlán finally comes into view, I am such a trembling ball of nerves and doubt that I am cross-eyed, and I can't see the beauty in anything at all. Central America isn't God's land anymore. It is cold and foggy and dangerous, and we are going around curves too fast.

The bus is overloaded. There are three people to every two-seater, people sitting on each other's laps, and people standing, scrunched up together all the way down the aisles from the fire exit to the front door. The driver is cackling, and seems to be acting drunk, and the people around me are stuck in a dead calm—completely unconcerned. His assistant climbs over people collecting money, and goes out the back door and scrambles up onto the roof while the bus is screaming and honking down the highway, passing trucks and other buses with even more stuff piled on the roof than ours. No matter how close we come to the cliff's edge or other vehicles, everyone else just rocks back and forth in their seats, leaning on each other when they need to. I am gripping the back of the seat in front of me, planning my escape, trying to think of the best position to be in if the bus goes over. I decide that the best thing to do is to just go limp. I have heard that injuries occur because people tense up and brace for impact, and that you have a better chance if you are relaxed. I scan the bus for emergency exits, and look for things I can grab onto if we roll over.

People all around me are laughing and smiling. Mothers are breast-feeding their babies. The woman next to me is asleep on my shoulder, with her black hair tickling my cheek.

It doesn't matter to them if they die today. They all

think they are going to heaven.

THREE VILLAGE TOUR

Since the 1970s, the Mayan village of Panajachel (Pana) has been a tourist haven. With expats, vegetarian restaurants, bookstores, backpacker hostels, and coffee shops, it is a town that attracts hippies, and fills multiple pages in any Guatemala guidebook. To say that it safer than Guatemala City is an understatement.

But I am so caught up in the fear of the capital, that I barricade myself in my hotel room out of habit. At dusk, I settle in to read, write in my journal, and go to sleep early. Out in the streets, however, the sounds of rowdy laughter, conversation in English, and bar music continue through the night. Around 11 p.m. I realize that the party isn't stopping, and that in Pana the rules are different. No one in Pana hides inside, terrified of crime. Instead, this town comes to life at night.

Timidly, I emerge from my room and wander downstairs to find many of the hotel guests playing cards and drinking wine in the lobby. Without hesitating, they ask me to join them. Before I know it, I find myself laughing, and realize it is the first time this has happened since I arrived. People ask about my Fulbright and I tell about the city, and in return, they tell stories about adventures through Mexico and Belize, and of innocent crimes committed to them in Pana—a stolen wallet in the market, being ripped off by a sly vendor, or clothes that never come back from the laundry. They also talk about how the locals are overly friendly, offering ridiculously low prices for hand-woven textiles, and smiling and saying "*buenas noches amiga*" as they pass by on the street. By midnight, tourists are taking to the streets in hoards, roaming up and down aimlessly, bar-hopping, drinking beer, singing, and laughing. The revelry continues until well past three in the morning.

Despite the late night and the wine, I wake up early. The air is dead still as I walk to the dock, and when I get there, Lake Atitlán is glassy-smooth like a mirror. Across the 26 kilometers of water, three volcanoes (Tolimán, San Pedro, and Atitlán) are so soft and purple that they appear to be sleeping. The tiny tuft of smoke spiraling up into the sky from Volcán Atitlán is the only sign of the furious heat and energy churning beneath the surface. I sit on the dock alone, resting, contemplating, and observing. It is the first moment of true peace I have had in nearly two months.

A man in shorts wanders down to the shore, leaves his towel on the beach, and wades into the water to bathe. Behind me, in the village, I hear the sounds of a Mayan town coming to life: the crowing of roosters, the soft puttering of the first motors and generators, the gentle swish of brooms, the tapping of pestles, and the clapping of hands making tortillas. Slowly, Panajachel awakes as vendors open stores and kiosks along Calle Santander, and the men operating the first boat taxis (*lanchas*) depart for other lake villages. Soon, the dogs are up and roaming around with sagging nipples flopping to and fro as they trot down the beach. As the sun rises higher in the sky, I stay on the dock and write in my journal while the lake slowly begins to stir with a gentle wind. Women in traditional dress appear at the shore, washing clothes on the rocks. *Lanchas* speed across the lake, stirring it up with their wake, and empty boatloads of people from the other towns onto the dock.

Lake Atitlán is like a secret garden—its own little encapsulated world—isolated from the rest of Guatemala by the steep ridge to the east and the three volcanoes to the west. There are thirteen different towns around the lakeshore, all of them populated mostly by Kakchiquel and Tzutujiil Maya. They are still highly self-sufficient communities, relying on the lake for fish, and on the crops that come from the terraced volcanic hillsides above their villages. For many of them, there is never a need to travel farther than Pana for supplies.

This lake itself is situated at 5,100 feet above sea level, and is a caldera, a massive crater that collapsed thousands of years ago in one of the world's largest volcanic eruptions—one that shot out 150 cubic kilometers of magma, with ash, rocks, and smoke reaching a height of 30 miles into the sky. The lake's true depth has never been measured, but it is said to be more than 1,000 feet deep and oral tradition speaks of its many spirits. In the *Popol Vuh*, the Mayan book of the dawn of life, Lake Atitlán is the sacred "lake of the south," one of four lakes that mark the sides of the Mayan world.

I stare at the crinkles and folds of the mountainsides and the slopes of the volcanoes, thinking about all the millions of years and the lava, and the water eroding the soil away, and the seasons changing to make everything look the way it does now. I think about the universe, and the planet, spinning around, and hurling through space at just the right distance from the sun for all this to be possible. I realize that now that I am an *atheist*, none of it is really God, just science at work.

After having tofu pizza for breakfast, I buy a ticket for a three-village boat tour, from a man who takes quite an interest in my freckles and the size of my arms.

"Wow!" he says, wrapping his fingers around my bicep and squeezing. "*Muy fuerte.*" Very strong.

I nod and laugh a little, even though I want to tell him

it is just fat.

"Why didn't you get the vaccine?" he asks, running his finger along my forearm.

"Vaccine?" I ask.

"For the disease. You get a shot in your arm, and then you don't get the spots."

I realize that he thinks my freckles are smallpox and I try to explain. He shrugs and hands me the ticket.

"50 Quetzales, *por favor.*"

And I pay him.

On the boat I meet Tabatha and Rolph, who tell me in thick French accents that they are from Quebec. I tell them about my anthropology studies, and with her nose in a *Lonely Planet* guidebook, Tabatha tells me authoritatively that the most interesting lake village on this tour will be Santiago Atitlán, the place where the Tzutujiil people first settled during pre-Columbian times, and where indigenous tradition is the most fully intact.

As we fly across the water that separates Pana from the first village, San Pedro la Laguna, they tell me all the places they've been, traveling by bus down from Mexico City, and planning to flying out of San Jose, Costa Rica in May. They swung around through the Yucatan and went to Merida and Playa del Carmen, then shot diagonally through Chiapas, stopping at San Cristobal de las Casas, crossed into Guatemala at La Mesilla, and chicken-bussed down through Huehuetenango and Xela. I listen in awe, and wonder whether I will have a chance to do the same, before my time here is over.

The water is so smooth and still that our *lancha* skips across it, like a pebble tossed across a pond. The boat itself has a deep fiberglass hull, bench seats down in the bottom, a roof across the top, and windows that can be covered with a clear plastic tarp. The driver stands at the stern, and runs the motor at full blast, not paying any attention to where he is going, distractedly talking in Tzutujiil to one of the passengers. Tabatha, Rolph, and I stand at the bow, feeling the wind and the sun on our faces, taking pictures of the volcanoes. Along the shoreline I see the Kakchiquel towns of Santa Cruz, Tzununá, San Marcos, and Jaibalito, tiny lakefront villages, with fishermen floating in the water, standing up in their *cayukos* and casting out nets, and women at the lakeshore washing clothes. Over the center of each town rises the white spire of a Catholic Church.

San Pedro la Laguna is tucked back into a lagoon in the northwest corner of the lake, at the base of the San Pedro volcano, protected by a rocky outcropping that juts out into the water. As we come around into a small harbor, the *lanchero* cuts back the motor, and we slide into a dock, bustling with happy chaos. Barefoot boys scramble around to tie off the lines, and help us out of the boat before asking us for 1 Quetzal.

Along the lakeshore, expats and wealthy creoles from the capital have built charming and elaborate restaurants, homes, and hotels with docks and beaches and garden terraces. When I step off the boat, the first things I notice are international restaurants, internet cafes, and signs for cappuccino. There are hippies along the street with handmade jewelry displayed on sun and moon and yin yang blankets, and one man with long, tangled dreads is twirling flaming poi. The sound of reggae bounces out of the cantinas, and the smell of garlic mixes in the air with marijuana.

In honor of my anthropological interests, I decide to find the church and the central market, which requires a steep hike up a cobbled road. The locals chuckle at me, and say "Hola, Gorda!" (hello Fatty) as I huff and puff up the sharply inclined slope, and try to sell me fresh lemonade and orange juice.

"No, gracias," I say at least a dozen times, smiling gently. I am slowly getting used to the descriptive names locals use to state the obvious. A blonde girl would be addressed as "Rubia" (blondie), while a bald man would jokingly be called "Pelado" (baldy), A skinny boy would be called "Flaco," and a dark-haired man would be called "Moreno." That leaves me with the very flattering "Gorda." While my size 14 is not something I'm proud of, I'm not tremendously overweight, so I can get over it without too much trauma. It doesn't take me too long to learn that "Chac," is the Tzutujiil word meaning the same thing.

When I arrive in the town center, I am in a different world. There are few tourists from the boat tours who make the climb, and thrill bubbles up inside me like the refreshing fizz of carbonation, as I realize I am in an *authentic* Mayan village. The Catholic Church is smack in the center of town, and is a massive, white building surrounded by topiary gardens. Out front is a statue of St. Peter holding a set of keys (presumably to the Pearly Gates of heaven), and beside him is the rooster from the Bible— the one that crowed three times while Peter denied Jesus on the day he was arrested.

Inside, the church is plainer than many I have seen in Guatemala City, but it is similar nonetheless. Long, wooden pews face the altar, and white and blue paper ribbons hanging down from the ceiling. I learn that the church is decorated this way for San Pedro Day, a day on which the Tzutujiil celebrate their heritage. Along the walls are paintings of the twelve apostles; in one alcove is a statue of Mary holding baby Jesus, with her head bowed over him; and in the back corner is a glass coffin with a replica of Jesus, wearing a crown of thorns and resting his head on a purple velvet pillow. Spread throughout the room are tables with candles, and from time to time, women wearing indigenous dress kneel in front of them, light new candles and pray harder than I've ever seen an American woman pray.

As I watch them, I can't help but feel a sense of loss.

After I leave, I stroll quickly through the market, and I am accosted by dozens of people trying to sell me fruits and trinkets. "*No, gracias*," I continue to repeat, again and again. As I walk guiltily away from each vendor without making any purchases, they shout lower and lower prices to me, until I am out of sight. I take mental notes for future bargaining. I don't take many photos, because when I see other tourists try to do so, the women turn their heads and cover their faces. Some successfully get shots by offering coins to children. But I am reluctant to do this because recently, in the north, a Japanese woman was murdered while taking photographs, and it is thought that the locals were afraid she wanted to kidnap their children.

I wander back down to the docks and have breakfast at a cafe on the water while I wait for the next boat to Santiago. Down here at the lakeshore, there are signs in English everywhere for Spanish schools, backstrap loom weaving lessons, kayak rental, horseback riding, and guided climbs of the volcano. Clustered around the main dock the restaurants boast Israeli, Nepalese, and English Pub food, with things like falafels, gadu gadu, and tomato basil soup on the menus. One café shows nightly movies. Tonight's is *Fear and Loathing in Las Vegas*, with Benicio del Toro and Johnny Depp.

As I order a fruit salad with yogurt, honey, and granola for breakfast, I scribble observations in my journal, and with each thing I write, more questions arise. My curiosity about the interactions and relationships between the local Mayan population and these expats is peaked, and I make a pledge to return to San Pedro soon. There is an inexplicable pull to the beauty of the lagoon, and I have to admit that the international food options, hippies, Hollywood movies, and English-speaking tourists make my fear and loneliness melt away like wax in the hot sun. Part of me wants to abandon the 3-village tour and stay here, but Tabatha says Santiago is interesting, so I will move on, with the promise of returning soon.

At the next table, a bedraggled white man with filthy hands orders French toast, then abruptly passes out, sprawling his arms across the table. When his food comes a few minutes later, the waitress looks at me timidly as if to ask whether she should wake him up. I shrug, and she leaves the food and walks away. Then, an old man with a long white beard and deep, drooping eyes, walks onto the terrace. "Charlie," he says. "If you don't eat that French toast soon, it's gonna be mine. Wake up, asshole!"

Charlie slowly raises his head and squints into the sun. "Shut-up, Dave. You mother-fucker," he says.

"Ey!" Dave shouts in a booming voice, turning towards the dock where tourists are unloading from one of the *lanchas*. "I got space cookies," he bellows. "Two flavors. Strong and stronger. Weed too. 100Q a bag." He turns back to Charlie. "You gotta lay off the shit, man. Stick with the easy stuff."

"Screw you," Charlie says. Looking as though his head weighs a hundred pounds, he moves the plate of food in front of him, picks up his fork, and closes his fist around his glass of juice. I watch him sway back and forth, staring at Dave with glazed eyes. Then his head nods once, and he collapses, his face smashing down into the French toast. The glass in his hand quivers and tips, soaking his hair and plate with orange and pulp.

"Charlie, you bitch," Dave says. "You ruined my breakfast."

The waitress comes back with a rag and apologetically wipes as much of the table as she can. As she gathers my plate, there is a glint of sadness in her eyes. "Too much *alcohól*," she says to me, shaking her head, but seeming unsurprised. "And drugs too."

From the water, Santiago Atitlán looks just like San Pedro—with a cluster of corrugated tin and cinderblock houses on a steep slope, around a central Catholic Church. There are *lanchas* pulling in and out of the docks, fishermen in *cayukos*, women washing their clothes on the rocks, and volcanoes towering overhead.

As our *lancha* skims towards Santiago through the cove

between the flanks of the San Pedro and Tolimán volcanoes, I can see that this Mayan village has a more organic quality to it than San Pedro or Pana, where there are plastics, and hot showers, and Diet Coke for the tourists. Instead, Santiago seems to fold itself into the landscape, the buildings and people growing up out of the earth like stalks of corn, instead of intruding upon it. As we come closer to the dock, the sound of Mayan chanting carries out eerily across the water, giving the place a sense of something sacred, indigenous, and ancestral.

Of these villages, Santiago is the only one I've heard of before coming to the lake, not just from Tabatha and her guide book, but from my studies of Mayan anthropology at the University. When I step onto the dock, women swarm around me like hornets, pushing textiles and masks and key chains towards my face. Everything they thrust at me smells like the earth, of indigo dye and soil. "Good price," they say in English, drawing their words out with thick accents. "How much you want to pay?"

"No, *gracias*," I repeat over and over again, pushing my way through. Other tourists from the boat tour are swallowed by the mob, and unwittingly reach for their wallets, buying souvenirs under pressure.

As soon as I break free from the crowd, I am surrounded by children reaching out towards me in curiosity and brushing their fingers along my freckled arms. Tabatha is right behind me with her guidebook open. "This is where Maximón is," she says.

"Who?" I say.

"Maximón. The Mayan god. There's a shrine here. We should go see it."

The kids perk up. "Maximón?" they say in chorus. "*Quieres ver a Maximón?* You want to see him? I take you there. Good price."

"Sure," I offer. "*Vamós.* Let's go." And we follow them as they giggle and race ahead down twisting dirt footpaths, between mud-brick houses with thatched roofs, and through courtyards filled with creeping ivy, zinnias, forsythias, and gigantic elephant ear leaves. Tabatha and I have to jog to keep up. Finally, we come through a rickety wooden gate and into an adobe house. "Shhhhh," the boys say, holding their fingers to their lips. They tiptoe towards the door and request 15 Quetzales for the entrance fee. We pay and are led inside.

The room is so dense with incense smoke I nearly stumble backwards when I walk through the door. Flickering candles decorate every surface, some melting in place and dripping globs of wax everywhere, and some in glass jars, etched with crosses or pictures of the Virgin Mary. The small space is filled with the wrinkled faces of dark-skinned Tzutujiil *ancianos* (elders) in layers of *traje,* and the walls seem to be painted with their shadows. Everyone has their eyes tightly closed, mumbling prayers. All the windows are covered with dark red and blue cloths, and only a small amount of daylight pinches its way through the cracks. The space and the ceremony going on in front of me appear to be authentic, and I dig through my bag for a camera and notepad.

"*No fotos,*" a woman hisses at me. "Unless you pay more." Embarrassed, I slip my camera back into my bag. A few other tourists are cross-legged in the corner, some bartering with the guy in charge about the price of taking pictures, and some refusing to sit down in the dirt because they are afraid of getting their clothes dirty. One European girl makes a show of splaying out her Goretex jacket on the ground for protection against the dust. I settle into a cross-legged position just in time for the ceremony to begin.

Beneath a picture of Jesus is the center of attraction: a wooden, life-sized carving of a man. This is Maximón. There is a lit cigarette hanging from a hole in his mouth, and yards of Mayan cloth are draped over the statue like clothing. An offering bowl sits in front of him, filled with Quetzales. As I scan the room more carefully, I notice dried herbs hanging from the ceiling and adobe walls, and pine needles and flower petals covering the floor. A young, local man enters the room, greets a few of the elders with kisses, kneels in front of the statue and begins praying feverishly.

According to Tz'utujiil legend, Maximón is the grand father of Santiago Atitlán, and is carved from the branch of a palo de pito tree (a tree that is said to speak wisdom and produce hallucinogenic visions when smoked). The shamans created him during pre-Hispanic times to rid the village of witches and sorcerers, whom he tricked by turning himself into an attractive young woman. The witches and sorcerers kidnapped the woman, who suddenly changed back into Maximón. They quickly let him go and ran to their houses, where they keeled over and died from vomiting and diarrhea.

At first, Maximón is said to have done his job and the town was freed from evil. But before long, he got out of hand and started killing indiscriminately, fooling the good people too. Death from vomiting and diarrhea had a grip on the whole town and the shamans were desperate. So, the shamans re-carved Maximón's face into the backside of his head, which they hoped would literally turn him around. To keep the deity appeased, they began to worship him, and bringing offerings of liquor, cigarettes, and money.

When the Spanish arrived, with their priests and armies, Tz'utujiil spirituality quickly changed. Catholicism integrated itself into daily life, and the large church was built in the center of town. Those who did not attend were punished, or killed. But the belief in Mayan gods and in Maximón was strong, and the Spanish could not break it—even when they told the people Maximón was really Judas from the Bible, that he had been responsible for the death of Jesus Christ. In demonstration of this, one priest even shot Maximón with a revolver and hacked him to pieces with a machete.

But under the cover of darkness, the Tzutujiil people still worshipped him, holding nighttime Pagan festivals during which cosmic dancers smoked the branches and grabbed his staff to harness his power and receive magical visions. In this way, many traditional Mayan beliefs have survived the centuries of Catholic, and now Evangelical and Protestant influence. A hybrid religion has been created, with people believing sincerely in the Christian God, and in Jesus Christ, but in many other gods as well. The statue in front of me and the ceremony represent the interesting balance that exists today in Guatemala, a unique brand of Catholicism, with a distinct Mayaness.

Today, Maximón is cared for by members of a Mayan brotherhood called the *Cofradía*. Each year a different elder takes him into their home, provides food for him at dinnertime, gives him clothes, and treats him as a member of the family. People come to the house every day to ask for Maximón's blessing. Men ask for wives and women ask for husbands. Some ask for life and some ask for money. It is considered a great honor to be the caretaker of Maximón. He has many names, and may be called the doctor, the angel, the branch that hits, the beyond, the astrologer, the great grandfather of the Tz'utujiil people, or *El gran abuelo maam*.

And here he is, five feet away from me, smoking a Marlboro red. On the floor next to him is a pint bottle of Venado Rum. Throughout the ceremony, a *Cofradía* member keeps the cigarette lit, and from time to time, removes it to pour rum in through the mouth hole. The praying man sits in front of the statue, rocking and singing with his eyes clenched shut. Behind him, a small, barefoot, and wrinkled *anciano* waves a bowl of incense and chants in a thick, guttural collection of consonants, creating a sound like singing and choking, at the same time.

At times, I find it hard to not to laugh out loud, and I try to be an observer, and to avoid the thoughts of how violence, fear, and oppression can make people believe so strongly in foreign ideas. But, here is yet another reminder of the influence of terror, of the man from Spain who came through 500 years ago and bullied everyone into believing.

On my side of the room, all the white tourists like me sit in the dirt cross-legged with their cameras in their laps, hypnotized by the chanting. We are becoming squint-eyed and sleepy from the heavy perfumed smoke, like we've been drugged. To my right, a hippie girl with long blond braids and patchwork skirt begins swaying with the rhythm and sobbing. On my left, a German woman is brushing dust off her waterproof jacket, looking utterly bored, like she is trying to keep from rolling her eyes.

It goes on like this for some time. Finally, the man with the incense starts chanting the same thing over and over again, and the praying man begins to cry. The word sounds like "ni-saang ... ni-saang ... ni-saang." It gets louder and louder, and all the Tzutujiil people in the room start chanting along. "Ni-saaaaaang ... ni-saaaaaang ... Ni-SAAAANG." People thrust their hands up in the air, squeeze their eyelids shut, and sway back and forth. "Ni-SAAAAANG ... Ni-SAAAANG."

Next to me, the German girl whispers something into the hippie's ear and she shrugs.

"What are they saying?" she asks me.

"I don't know," I say.

It gets louder. "NI-SAAAAAANG ... NI-SAAAAANG ... NI-SAAAAANG."

Then everything stops abruptly and there is silence—a long silence, and nobody moves. Finally, a rooster crows in the courtyard. Then, as if awakened by the cue, the kneeling man opens his clenched fist, and places a photograph of a rusted blue pick-up truck upon the flower petals and pine needles that carpet the floor at Maximón's feet.

"Oh," the German girl whispers. "Nissan." She suppresses a giggle.

The man leans forward and kisses the doll's forehead. When he leans back, his hands and lips are shaking and an old woman emerges from the shadows, whispers something into his ear, and places an arm around his shoulder. He wipes his tears, then they both cross themselves in the Catholic style and leave the room arm in arm, hunched together as though neither one of them have the strength to stand on their own. When someone finally pulls back the curtain from across the door, the sunlight comes spilling into the room, and all the smoke from the incense goes billowing out.

"That was crazy," I hear the German girl say, once we were outside. She snorts and shakes her head. "I can't believe they went through all that crap, just for a stupid, beat-up, pick-up truck."

CRASH

By the time I return to my apartment in Guatemala City on Sunday evening, I am physically and mentally exhausted. I slide under the covers with my journal and realize that everything has changed. I look over at the bible sitting on the nightstand. Beside it, in a glimmering pile, is a delicate, gold necklace—a cross from Costa Rica that, until now, I have worn around my neck every day.

It is strange to turn out the light and close my eyes without praying, and I'm not sure what to do with myself. Even though I am tired, my head is spinning with images, sounds, and smells from my weekend in Atitlán. As hard as I try, I can't fall asleep.

After an hour I give up, get up, and settle at my desk to do some research and reading on the two villages where I will be doing my fieldwork. Rabinal and San Miguel Chicaj are two towns in the central part of Guatemala known for their textiles, artisans, and adherence to pre-Columbian traditions, folklore, and dance. Both were founded in the early 1500s by the Spanish Fray, Bartolomé de Las Casas, as a base for his proselytizing. Rabinal will become my home base as soon as my classes at UVG are over, and my goal there is to study the *huipiles* (Fig. 1).

These are simply-shaped, but elaborately-decorated tunics that represent the individual histories of each village. As years have passed, the designs on these *huipiles* changed to represent events that occured in the lives of villagers. The idea behind my Fulbright proposal is to study the designs and oral histories over the past fifty years. From this, I am supposed to draw some kind of fascinating anthropological conclusion

The details of my fieldwork are loosely in place. I have arranged through the Ixchel Museum to go and live in Rabinal with a woman who has a sister in San Miguel Chicaj. She will be my ticket into the hearts and minds of the *ancianos*, and will serve as my translator, as I interview them and record their oral history. I will have to gain their trust and record everything. I will take thousands of photographs and collect samples, and learn how to weave using the traditional methods.

The region in which these two villages are located is not close to any major tourist destinations. They do not see many outsiders and I know they will be mistrusting. This will be my biggest challenge. As I scan my literature, I read that in one international incident, nearby in San Cristobal Verapáz, a woman was beaten into a coma for photographing children in 1994. The locals feared she wanted to kidnap them, and raise them as her own. As I continue, I find more terrifying accounts of the locals' fear of foreigners. They are not without reason. In the violence of the 1980s, the military hit the area quite hard. The population was decimated as hundreds of people simply disappeared overnight. Villages were wiped off the map in one fell swoop. Most recently, the excavation of a mass burial site, has sparked violence towards anthropologists.

In Rabinal today, there is little access to running water, phone service, or internet; bus service is infrequent; and in my homestay I will be sleeping on a bed made of straw. As I reflect on my weekend in the beauty of Lake Atitlán, my stomach churns with apprehension and the loneliness of such isolation. The thought of truly roughing it for five months (in an area known for massacres, violence towards tourists, where no one will be speaking English, where I will not even be able to call home, and where I will have trouble finding potable water and food that won't make me sick) has suddenly lost a lot of its appeal. I stare down at my books, deflating like a punctured balloon.

In a moment of inspiration and desperation, I hammer out an email to my contact at the Institute of International Education in New York (the organization that granted my proposal and awarded my Fulbright). In it, I ask if it would be possible to change my project, and propose a new idea: an examination of the tourist culture of Lake Atitlán, immersion in the town of San Pedro la Laguna, and a study of how the resident expats and drug culture have affected and changed the Tzutujiil way of life.

Finally, I go to sleep, hopeful.

In the morning, there is a response. *The grant is really about your experience in the country. How you use your Fulbright money, and the project you complete are entirely up to you. Good luck.*

At the University, my thoughts bounce around like the birds that keep landing on the windowsill. I struggle to pay attention, wondering how on earth I will make it to the end of the semester in May. We are only halfway through March, and my motivation is dwindling rapidly. The classes cover material I already know, and for the first time in my life, grades and credits mean nothing.

I plod through each day, sometimes skipping class in favor of doing more meaningful research on my own. When I do go to class, all I can focus on is the way the professors have no control of the classroom and how students answer their cell phones during lecture, crunch on noisy bags of potato chips, and throw paper airplanes. I gaze out the window at the volcanoes, feeling like I have senioritis, and it is days before graduation.

So, I start traveling to San Pedro on the weekends to set up my new home base. I find a hotel with a view of the lake, a "kitchen" and a hot shower, where I can stay for $60 a month. I bargain the owner down to $40 by paying for three months up front. Every weekend, as I make the trip from Guatemala City, I bring a few more of my belongings, slowly moving to the lake, trip by trip. I get to know some of the expats, and develop a taste for certain menu items at their restaurants. I drink coffee in the mornings at D'Noz, on a balcony overlooking the main dock. I people watch.

I am back and forth from Lake Atitlán a lot, and am slowly getting used to the terror of Chicken Bus rides. I have learned to accept my fate each time I climb on board. I have started to tell myself "I might die today, and if I do, I've lived life to the fullest." The only thing that nags at me is the thought of heaven.

Then, one day on the intercity bus on the way to the University, I see a girl who does not look Guatemalan. Around her neck is a strange necklace, a huge blue and black beetle, clinging two inches below her throat. We stare at each other for a while, and when we both stand to get off at the same stop, she turns to me and says, "Hi. I'm Maureen."

I introduce myself, in English.

Maureen is from North Carolina, and is studying abroad for a semester at UVG. She is an anthropology student. As she tells me this, I can't believe we haven't met sooner. I ask about her necklace and she says that it is a project for her anthropology class, and she has more she has made out of beetles, butterflies, and spiders. She is trying to sell them. We both have to get to class, but we agree to meet at the bakery across the street afterwards.

Maureen and I become fast friends, and we meet at the bakery two or three times a week. One day when she reaches out and touches my arm, I realize that it is the first time since I arrive that I have had physical contact with another person. In my loneliness, I cling to her like she is a piece of driftwood on the ocean. I think that maybe she could be my best friend. She is different from the Guatemalan girls, who all wear too-tight jeans, and too much perfume, and seem to care only about being pretty and having boyfriends and getting married. I have tried to make friends with them, but simply can't connect. But Maureen is wild and free-spirited in her appearance. She is beautiful and un-tamed, without the make-up, designer clothes, and three-inch heels all the other girls around us think they need. Instead, she wears Birkenstocks and quick-dry clothing, and carries a Nalgene, like me.

We start traveling together on the weekends. We finish the food on each other's plates, get caught in the rain, pack light, and keep an eye out for each other. We visit towns that are off-the-beaten-path, and talk about deep stuff, like the existence of God, and the meaning of life, and societal roles. We try to talk only in Spanish sometimes, for practice. I find myself wanting to be like her—so in love with the traveling life that settling in one place for too long might always be impossible. We want to spend our entire lives on the road, to see it all, set foot on every continent, in every country on the planet. Maureen has passion. I decide that part of why I'm here in Guatemala is to find something to be truly passionate about, and to carry it around with me the way she does, bursting with energy and life. Mostly I want to be like her because she is happy on her own, as a woman alone.

One weekend, Maureen goes to Lake Atitlán with her anthropology class, and I choose instead to travel to Rio Dulce on the Caribbean coast. There, I discover a completely different side of Guatemala, with retired American sailors, and Garifuna Rastafarians, beach bars, wet heat, hammocks, and savory sea bass. It is refreshing to tote my pack around, to challenge myself to sleep in a bungalow filled with spiders, and to feel the independence of traveling alone again. On Monday morning, back in Guate, I call Maureen, bursting to tell her about my trip.

On the other end of the line, her voice is weak and trembling.

"Are you okay?" I say.

"Um … not really," she chokes. "No one heard the other boat coming until it was right on top of us." The crash killed at least two people, she says, but it might have been more.

Her story goes like this: Two *lanchas*, with their noses so high out of the water they couldn't see in front of them, collided at high speed in the middle of the lake. Maureen's boat had turned away at the last moment to avoid a head-on crash. The other boat crashed across the back of her *lancha*. As it smashed into them, it ripped off a woman's arm. Maureen was thrown against the wall, breaking a rib. She lost consciousness. The boat she was on sank quickly. When she awoke, she was lying in the hull of the surviving *lancha*. The woman with her arm torn off was bleeding profusely. Neither her boat's captain or his assistant were there. She asked about them. They had been standing directly in the path of the oncoming *lancha*, and were killed on impact. Their bodies had gone down with the boat, to join the thousands of other corpses in the unmeasured depths of the great grave that is Lake Atitlán.

"It sank so fast," she says, "and it was like no one even cared about making sure everyone was accounted for. There is no concern for safety, even after the fact. I actually saw the boat hit them. Just telling the story makes me want to throw up."

The surviving *lancha* had headed for San Pedro.

"And no one cared. All they could say was '*asi es la vida*'—you know—'that's life'." Maureen's voice shakes with anger. "It's like they just don't value life at all. That woman who lost her arm—they took her to shore and they just let her lay there. They rushed me up to the doctor because I was white, and they knew I could afford to pay for it. When I got back down to the docks, she was still laying there in a pool of blood, and no one cared."

I ask if she is going to be okay. "Do you need anything?"

"Nah, I'll be okay." She sighs. "I broke a couple of ribs, but I'll be fine." She pauses. "But I was thinking, Cindy, if you had gone with me, you probably would have been sitting right beside me on that boat. That could have been *you* who lost your arm."

After that phone call, all I want to do is pray, but I can't.

At night, I torment myself with fear, thinking about vulnerability and how it really could have been me, or her, or how any of us can die at any time leaving everything in our path unresolved and meaningless. After all, what's the point of all this searching, when we all die in the end anyway?

I convince myself that Guatemala is out to get me.

Whether it will kill me, or make me stronger, I don't know. All I know was that the crash seems to be the first in a series of events in which I am confronted by death. Suddenly I start to see death everywhere. I ride past bus crashes where there is blood on the windows. I see a homeless man face-up with his eyes open on the sidewalk in Zone 1, who has been there long enough for rigor mortis to set in. I feel it chasing me and I imagine the sound of footsteps following me in the twilight as I race home from the University to beat the darkness. I see it in the armed guards who stand like statues in front of every business. I see it in the eyes of the Tzutujiil people. I read it in the newspaper. I read it in the history books. Every time I close my eyes, I see bodies. Bodies strewn across the hills, bodies at the bottom of the lake, buses overturned and people with blood streaming down their faces. And then that word circling through my mind—dead. Dead. Dead. Dead. Dead.

In April, my life in Guatemala City means dust on everything. My books. My pillow cases. My shower floor. My lips. My lungs. My brain. I can't think straight. I am too busy being dirty, grimy, sweaty all the time, feeling like living in the city has violated me somehow. I shower three times a day, just to feel some semblance of home. It becomes an obsessive ritual, being clean. I buy expensive glycerin soaps in Pana that smell like sandalwood and patchouli, and I scrub my feet with a pumice stone that I find one weekend, floating in Lake Atitlán. I shave my legs, even though no one is there to touch them, and I slather on lotion and paint my toenails.

But no matter how much I exfoliate and scrub and lather and soak, day after day, I can not clean Guatemala City from my skin. When I leave my house, it is like I am in full costume, with my make-up, and ironed clothes, and styled hair. The street is my stage—the place where I put on an act every day, pretending to be confident and to know where I am going, like I am *Guatemalteca*—immune to the hissing, and the stares. I do such a good job of this that one day, someone pulls up beside me and asks for directions. When men yell at me from across the street, I ignore them. When they talk about me on the bus, I let them think I can't understand, and that they don't bother me. I wear my whiteness like a mask—letting it confuse them, so they don't know whether I am from here or there. But there is an emptiness to it. Each day of pretending makes me long more and more for a place that could actually feel like home. Where there is no question whether or not I belong there, and people just accept me as I am—dirty feet, fat arms, freckles and all.

It is so dry in Guate that my skin cracks open and bleeds. My hair becomes a crinkled, noisy mess, and I cut it short and sell my blow dryer to a vendor in the market. My nose is perpetually sunburned and peeling, and I give up on make-up because the skin on my chin is dry and flaking, probably from all the cosmetics. By the middle of the month, Maureen convinces me that I should do what I want. I can't stand looking at all the dead brown hillsides anymore, and I drop out of the University.

Leaving the city behind on a chicken bus, I look down on the haze of sprawling skyscrapers and shantytowns. From up above, the whole place is parched, dusty, dry, covered in a blanket of thick yellow smog—plagued by a deep insatiable thirst.

Maureen and I fall out of touch. The crash rattled her, and I assume she has headed home.

Author's note: Maureen and I ran into each other in Boulder, Colorado at a bluegrass house party in 2011. We live within thirty minutes of each other and have since renewed our friendship. We speak frequently about our respective anthropological journeys in Guatemala and how they changed our lives forever.

SAN PEDRO LA LAGUNA

The crossing from Pana is terrifying. I keep imagining Maureen's accident. Since the crash, they now have boys standing on the bows of all the boats, watching the water up ahead, and motioning to the captain if something is in the way. It is a genuine and surprising effort by the *lancheros* to be more safety conscious. Of course, the kids aren't always diligent, wandering around the boat, turning around and tying knots in a length of rope, leaving me with the need to peer out over the bow from where I sit in the front, just to make sure we don't run over any fishermen.

There is still a sense of aloofness about these new safety regulations, and no one will talk honestly about the accident. They want their money, and have no desire to spread rumors that will drive tourists away. I try to understand their motivation.

When I ask the captain about Maureen's crash, he looks me in the eyes, smiles, and lies to me. "It was just a small accident, and no one died," he says. "I think there were some minor injuries."

I reach up to untie the life vest from over my head. At the very least, my body will float and it can be sent home to my parents.

But the captain starts shouting from the back of the

boat and wagging his finger at me. "No lifejackets now!" he says. "Only for emergency. You untie one, they all fall down."

As we come out into the center of the water, the wind picks up and we crash over five-foot waves, our backsides smashing down on the hard wooden seats. I clutch the bench and tell myself that the probability of two fatal boat accidents happening in the same month is very low. I begin examining the structural integrity of the fiberglass hull, and planning my escape route if the worst should happen, and both boats sink, without a chance to grab a life vest, leaving no one to rescue me. I try to think up ways to fight off hypothermia during the swim to shore if that ends up being my only option. If we go down right in the middle of the crossing, I will have 13 kilometers to swim. Almost eight miles. I am a strong swimmer, but I have never swum that far before. Night would surely come and go before I reach a shore, and it would be hopeless. With the water being as cold as it is, and the afternoon wind and five foot swells, survival will depend on me keeping my body moving, no matter how tired I get. If I don't, I'll drown.

I can't imagine what it must have been like for Maureen that day, with that boat coming out of nowhere. Watching that woman lie on the lakeshore afterwards, bleeding, without her arm. Those two men (and maybe more—no one knows) were killed instantly, swallowed by the lake, without anyone seeming concerned about safety or death at all when it was all over. And even though I wasn't there, the accident has haunted me—and it isn't just thinking that it could have been me on that boat, but that death can sneak up on you anywhere, at any time, ready or not.

In the States, we are so protected from death that we really only associate it with disease and old age and the occasional car crash or freak accident—not with instants in time where everything goes wrong because people have seen so much death already that it doesn't matter. That they have no concern for safety in the first place. The only funerals I've attended were for my grandparents, who had all been sick for years, and for my Uncle Tom who died from multiple sclerosis. Sure, I've seen those flashing lights on the highway, and have been there when the traffic slows down because everyone is craning their heads to look at a smashed up car, and I have seen the crosses on the side of the road, and I have had my own close calls. But I have never really seen what death does to someone, just police tape and flashing lights, and strategically positioned emergency vehicles blocking the view. Guatemala is the first time in my life that death has been right there, out in the open, reminding me of my mortality every day. Here, people are so used to it that their faces seem permanently hardened to stone.

I had seen my first dead body at the very beginning of my trip, in January. He was lying face down in the street in Antigua, with people stepping around him, not even paying attention. I told some of the students at school about it, and they shrugged and said, "So what? What's the big deal about that? We see dead bodies all the time." They nodded absently like four or five deaths in a day would be no big deal. They read the papers without feeling like Guatemala City was a death trap. They went out at night, even though their own brothers had been kidnapped from out of their cars, and murdered in the streets. "These things happen," they said, shrugging their shoulders. "*Asi es la vida.*" That's life. They acted like they had given up on being afraid a long time ago.

Stepping off of the *lancha* and looking up at the San Pedro volcano hovering softly in the evening sky, I feel a flicker of heat surge through me. My body fills with the warmth and tingle of energy, excitement, and passion. I breathe the air in, relaxing with the smell of smoke, banana bread, horse manure, and the pulpy bite of wet coffee beans.

"Hola, amiga," a boy says, recognizing me. He offers to carry my bag to my hotel.

On the surface, relations between the hundreds of backpackers and expats at the lake seems almost too good to be true. There is so much outward kindness. So much thanks for the money we bring to their town. But is there any resentment? Doesn't there have to be? This is my new project—to find out if the "most beautiful lake in the world," a place that seems so friendly to tourists on the surface, has a dark side as a result of globalization and tourism.

Dropping out of UVG and changing my project gives me a renewed sense of independence, empowerment, and relief. My homesickness and paranoia melt away. I decide to relax, to put less pressure on myself, and enjoy life a little. In San Pedro, maybe I can fit in, make a few real friends, and maybe even find a cute backpacker guy to mess around with. I want to party, to learn more about this mixed-up religion, and to analyze my fear and theirs. I am curious about what the Tz'utujiil people have faith in, about what carries them through each day in the midst of poverty, warfare, disease, the death of their children, and oppression. Is it Catholicism? God? Communion and prayer on Sundays? Or is it their belief in energy of the lake and the earth, the cycle of life, and the spirits of their ancestors?

I feel the energy of Atitlán, though I don't know what it is I am feeling. I want to be open to everything, to somehow find a way to feel spiritual, to understand the universe again. To do this, I make myself a blank slate.

My room is in a little purple hostel called Posada Xetawal. The owners are Pedro and Catarina—gentle, smiling Tz'utujiil people whose eyes light up when they see me. They offer to let me keep milk and cheese in their fridge, and they take care of spiders in my room and snakes in the shower. One day, I accidentally leave my bag behind at their store and their son chases me down the street to give it back. It seems like maybe San Pedro is safe enough that I don't have to be afraid anymore.

There are so many screwed up expatriates in town that I seem straight-edge and normal compared to most of them, and don't have to worry at all about my image, or keeping it together, or being overly nice to make friends. The readily available drugs, the affordable liquor, the late nights, and the lazy hangover mornings spent swinging in hammocks are the draw. People come to town for the island feel, and disappear into a mind-altering haze, forgetting about their old lives, and sticking around until they get itchy to move on again.

As a child of the 1980s, and DARE programs that dared me to say no to drugs, I keep my distance from the drug scene, though I do drink and stay out late more than I would at home. Instead, I spend my time cultivating my health of body and mind, taking long walks, horseback riding along the flanks of the volcano, and swimming and kayaking in the lake. Most days, I meditate and go to yoga class, then lay out on the rocks during the heat of the day, letting myself bake in the sun. In the afternoons, I borrow worn copies of literary classics from lending libraries, and rock in hammocks, and drink banana *licuados*, and read about the cold winters in 18th century Russia, and forbidden love in 19th century England, and peyote, and the teachings of Don Juan. At night I go out and see movies at D'Noz Restaurant and have dinner there, and make temporary friends with the backpackers, and end up in their hotel rooms listening to them sing and play strange instruments. Most people I meet are just passing through and disappear as soon as I start to like them. *Nothing lasts forever*, I tell myself. *Everybody leaves.* I get used to it. There are only a handful who stay longer than a few weeks— expats from Australia, South Africa, England and Israel who have made San Pedro home. They are a more difficult crowd to win over, but I get a job at D'Noz and it seals the deal. I make about 75 cents an hour, and I'm one of them now.

San Pedro is a town of constant noise, with a perpetual sense of things always going on all around me, of time moving forward, even when I am lying in bed trying to calm my mind and pretend that the world is standing still. It is at once a self-sufficient Mayan town where all the locals wake up at dawn to make tortillas and take baths in the lake, and a late-night party town, where the hippies and expats wander home dazed, drunk, and stumbling into bed in the pitch dark night. The town itself throbs with loud music and the noise and heat of life. It rises and falls, coming and going like a tide, like an undulating symphony that will only end if the moon falls out of the sky. There are fleeting moments of quiet, after all the bars are closed, and people are done wandering home through the streets, when all I can hear are chickens rustling around under the coffee trees, pecking at trash, and the dogs barking as though warning of intruders—as though they are trying to remind the locals that some of us in town aren't really supposed to be here.

Whether I am supposed to be here or not, San Pedro wraps around me like a pair of strong arms. It feels right in so many ways. I meditate with the hippies on the rocks. I drink infusions made from herbs grown by the cycle of the moon. I get up before sunrise every morning and take the boat to San Marcos, for 7:00 Hatha yoga in a wooden pyramid temple. I shop at the market and start living off of papaya and pineapple and watermelon, and losing weight. I challenge myself to spend only what I make in a day at D'Noz, to live within my means at less than $20 a week. My pants are all suddenly too big, and I have to commission two new pairs from an indigenous man in Pana. They are my first handmade Guatemalan hippie pants, with baggy legs, and textiles for the cuffs and pockets.

Once I have the pants, all I have to do is stop brushing my hair and shaving my armpits, and I am *in style*.

All the expats are wearing them. It is the outward proof that we have been in Guatemala long enough to need new clothes. It makes us "hardcore." It almost makes us "locals". The ones who are really serious about proving themselves have whole outfits—textile purses and textile shirts, necklaces with Peruvian beads and seashells and amber that the South American and Mexican backpackers sell on the street, and leather sandals, and pants just like mine. I want to be like them. All hippie and vegetarian, and glowing with health. I want to look good in flowing clothes, make jewelry from amber, and wear white without getting it dirty.

Compared to Guatemala City, San Pedro represents unrestrained freedom. I can stay out late and walk home alone after midnight without worrying. I can leave my purse behind somewhere and go back for it an hour later and it will still be there. I can say hello to anyone I pass on the street. I don't always have to lie and say I am married. I swim in the lake everyday and carry a plastic basket to the market, just like the *San Pedranas*. I wear my bathing suit under a tank top, and my sarong everywhere. I walk around town barefoot or in flip flops. I get a deep suntan that makes all my freckles blend together, and my hair turn blonde. It only takes a couple of weeks before I settle in completely. When I started washing my clothes at the lakeshore with the Tz'utujiil women, they laugh at my technique and show me how and say, "*Tú eres pura Pedrana.*" You are a pure San Pedro woman.

Fulbright phase I: Immersion in local culture. Check.

The town itself is a portrait of Guatemala, full of contradiction: poverty and wealth; earthy dark skin and porcelain white; corn tortillas and Cocoa Puffs; Mayan ceremony and Christianity; locals speaking Tz'utujiil, Spanish, English, German, and Israeli; old folks unable to communicate with their grandchildren because they never needed Spanish until a few years ago. It is a place where two entirely different dimensions are crashing together.

Half of the town is frozen in time—with adobe houses and corrugated tin roofs and chickens in the yards, and men who go out to work the fields at dawn every morning. And the other half is boiling with energy, scattered with tourists and growing at record pace, with internet cafes, cappuccino, and Peanut M&Ms, and hotels with hot water and cable television springing up like sprouts in fertile soil. These worlds are layered on top of each other, woven together in bright colors, like Mayan cloth, together creating a spellbinding allure that keeps me here, making me never want to leave.

The travelers who don't come for the drugs come to volunteer, or learn Spanish. Some start environmental campaigns to "save the lake," even though none of the locals knew that it needed saving until now. Others volunteer at the San Juan school for handicapped children, and some get jobs at restaurants serving backpackers, where they don't need to learn Spanish at all. Most of them come through quickly, but some stay long enough to take a few weeks at a Spanish school, do a home-stay with a local family, and make connections that are hard to leave in the end.

The most successful expats are business-minded, like the European couple who owns D'Noz. With their restaurant and internet café, Dean (from the U.K.) and Monica (from Holland) have found a way to make good money, support the town, and provide work for the locals, and a haven for weary travelers. Many of the expats are not so business-minded. Instead, they are lazy, hollowed-out shells of hippies, who try to make money here and there, but end up distracted by the promise of getting high and drunk, and twirling flaming batons in the streets. They walk around aimlessly, sleep until mid-afternoon, and show up at the bar every night to purchase full bottles of Tequila and snort lines of cocaine off the back of the toilet.

At first, I don't smoke marijuana or do other drugs

because I am an anthropologist and I am in town on serious business. I have work to do. Interviews to conduct. Photos to take. Volumes to learn about the lake cultures. I feel like there are great expectations of me, too. Surely my college professors who helped me get this grant are waiting for some kind of journal article for *American Antiquity* or *Granta,* for me to give a slide show and a lecture about my project. I am going to have to at least fake it, and I don't want to fake it entirely because Fulbright grants are prestigious, and they chose me, and I don't want to let them down. True, no one is giving me a grade, or making me publish anything, but they gave me money with confidence and sent me into the world, and I feel obligated to put it to anthropological use. Somehow. So I continue to religiously take field notes in my journal every day.

After a month of settling into San Pedro, and allowing my body and mind to recover from the trauma of Guate, I get back on track with my research by taking weaving lessons. I tell my teacher, Olimpia, that I want to learn how to weave in the traditional way, on a backstrap loom, like the *Pedranas* do. We go to the market together and I pick out six colors to make a scarf. As I sift through the selection of colors, Olivia stands beside me, squeezing my shoulders, and saying, "*ay, que bonita,*" when I match iridescent colors together. She frowns when I choose earth tones. "Brighter," she says, matching neon blue with orange. "More color is prettier."

Back at her house, we string the threads across a low wheel with vertical sticks coming out of the top. The device stands about nine inches high. Beside me is another oblong wheel, which we wrap the thread around so it will unwind as we string it around the sticks. We make layers of color, wrapping all the thread around the sticks, with her daughter Leslie peering over my shoulder, and leaning on me while I work. Leslie says that by at the age of four, she already knew how to weave. "*Un poquito,*" she says, blushing. A little bit.

Each time my threads get tangled up both Leslie and Olimpia lean over and work the knots with the patience of nuns, prying apart tiny strings with their fingernails, laughing at me and draping their bodies over me with affection. Their touch is so warm, their bodies so soft and light against me. Ah, the sweetness of physical contact, after months of so little. Leslie lays her head on my shoulder, and I feel something inside me crack and soften. I reach up and tousle my hand in her black, silky hair.

In traditional Mayan culture, girls are taught to weave from the day of their birth, when weaving sticks are placed in their hands as part of the birth ceremony. Weaving is considered to be one of women's most important tasks. To fail at weaving is equivalent to failing as a woman. Anthropologist Brenda Rosenbaum says in an essay, "The instruments used for spinning and weaving, and the clothes produced with them defined women; just as weapons, a loincloth, and cape defined men … weaving is to battle, as woman is to man" (*Mayan Women, Weaving and Ethnic Identity: A Historical Essay*, 1999). The art of weaving is passed from mother to daughter, and is a very important part of the bond they share. Boys share a similar bond with their fathers, but instead of weaving sticks, they are given a hoe at birth and told that it will be their job to learn to work the earth, and to help provide for the family and the community.

In modern times, the use of traditional dress, (*traje*) is often limited to women, and defines them not only as Mayan, but connects them to a particular village—the dress from each one being so distinctive that even I am beginning to recognize the colors and patterns that belong to certain villages. Men throughout most of Guatemala no longer wear indigenous dress. Without it they can disguise themselves as *ladinos* and get jobs in the capital. Only the older men around Lake Atitlán can be seen wearing the traditional sashes and checkered pants they have always worn. Anyone under the age of 50 wears jeans and t-shirts, except when they wear *traje* for ceremonial reasons. The loss of traditional dress is one of the most visible ways that Guatemala is changing from globalization and tourism. Not only are both men and women turning to western dress because of the anonymity it provides them, but those who do continue to use *traje* have stopped dying threads in the traditional way, with crushed indigo and cochineal, and often use mass-produced synthetic fabric instead. This is why there is such a flurry of anthropological excitement over textiles in Guatemala. This kind of weaving is a disappearing art. It is something that is not being passed down the way it once was. Only a few girls today are like Leslie, lucky enough to learn the old techniques before they die away completely.

Weaving lessons get me in the doors of people's houses, and give me time to sit for hours and talk with them. It is a doorway to the underbelly of San Pedro, and to the part most tourists don't get the chance to see. Shamans. Bonesetters. Curses. Witchcraft. Murder. Drugs. I get all this when Mayan families let me into their homes.

Olimpia's house is sparsely furnished. In fact, it is almost empty. She lives in the center of town, at the top of the hill, in an unfinished cinderblock cube, sandwiched between a row of other homes and shops, accessed by a narrow alleyway, littered with trash and smelling like urine. The bathroom is a green, cement, bucket-flush toilet, with an oil drum full of water for the reservoir. Everything else in her home is gray, cement, and unpainted. In the main room, where our weaving lessons are held, there is no furniture. Just weaving sticks scattered across the floor, and hooks in the ceiling, and one wooden chair, though Olimpia and Leslie don't use it. They just kneel on the ground for hours. The only thing hanging on the wall is a crucifix.

Once the threads for my scarf are laid out, Olimpia takes them off the winding board and soaks them in a solution of corn and water.

"This will make the threads strong," she says, tugging on them. "So the fabric will not rip." We slide sticks in between the gaps, and attach one end of the cloth to a hook on the wall. The other end we attach to a leather sling that will wrap around my waist. At the end of my first lesson, the backstrap loom is ready, and we take it up to the roof and stretched it out to dry in the sun.

I come back a few days later and learn how to caste the shuttle back and forth between the threads, smashing them down with a stick, laying row upon row. It is a surprisingly strenuous process, and tests my arm and stomach muscles more than they have been tested since my days of lugging archaeology gear across long, grassy fields.

While I work, Olimpia began spontaneously talking. "You are from the United States?" she asks me.

"Yes. From the east coast."

"Is it big?" she says. "Your country?"

"Yes. It's pretty big. Five thousand kilometers across."

Her eyes grow wide, as though the U.S. is a mystical land in some medieval fairy tale. "Really? Is it far from here?"

"Five hours or so by airplane."

"*Volando*," she whispers. Flying. "When I was a child, I used to think it was so close. The next village. Just there." She gestures north.

"The earth is very big," I tell her, quietly.

She nods. "Five years ago, there was no electricity in San Pedro," she says. "There was only one school. Only a couple of hotels. Only *comedores*—no nice restaurants like now. There was nothing at the lakeshore. It was all fields. When the Evangelists came, that is when everything started to change." She tells me how they used to stand on the corners and preach to everybody. And how they came with big groups from the U.S. and started building schools and churches. How they brought dentists and doctors who roamed around town working for free. How five years ago, she had never seen a computer, watched a television, or drunk a Pepsi. "How fast it is changing," she says. "I am only 22 years old, and I feel like an *anciana* for how fast it is changing."

I am stunned to hear her age. The same as mine. Yet her face is sunken in and weary. Her hair has streaks of gray running through it. She has wrinkles in the corners of her eyes, and melanoma on her cheeks, and her daughter is already five. If I had guessed, I would have put her at almost twice that age. At least forty.

The life expectancy for Mayan women ranges depending on the area, from 44 years in the Peten Jungle and Chiapas Mexico, to 66 in the Western Highlands. The weight of hard labor and heavy grief has taken its toll, and everyone looks years older than they are, with sunspots and deep wrinkles carved into young faces, and silver hair on everyone over 40. Even children look haggard sometimes. Yet everyone is so strong: carrying loads twice their weight, balanced on their heads for miles; kneeling for hours; carrying children while they work in the fields; going barefoot for months when there is no money for even the dingy plastic shoes on sale for 1 Quetzal in the market; waking up at 4:00 every morning to make tortillas for their husbands to take to the fields.

And unlike me, they never complain about a thing.

KAYLA

Coming back down the hill to the gringo side after my weaving lesson is always slightly shocking to my senses, and at the same time, slightly reassuring. There is a completely different atmosphere at the docks than up in town. Cafes and bars, and tourists eating and sitting at plastic tables on patios in the sun. It is like summer vacation down here. The expats wander around the streets, some of them on their way to and from work at one of the restaurants, and some of them lurking, bothering tourists, trying to sell them drugs.

"Space cookies," a familiar voice bellows one afternoon. "We've got galactic and super-galactic today." Dave strolls down the street towards me, where I am climbing the steps into D'Noz Restaurant. Today he is wearing a white robe and walking with a cane, looking even more like Moses than before.

"Do you try to look like Moses on purpose?" I ask him.

He laughs and shakes his cane at me. "Cut an old man some slack, eh? Holiness is good for my image. It keeps the fucking cops away."

I work at D'Noz almost every day. Dean has been in San Pedro for almost as long as the town has had electricity, and helped fuel the first influx of expats to the town with his restaurant—a place that gave them jobs, serves baguettes and salads and stir fries and eggs, and shows movies every night. It is a true culinary oasis (in a country not particularly known for its fine cuisine). Eating at D'Noz is like feeling the comfort of home, but still being immersed completely in Guatemala. It is right on the water, with bougainvillea spilling down off the balcony; basil, coriander, and cilantro growing in the garden; and a wide-open view of a rock formation called the Indian Nose. It is where I check my email, borrow books, and play chess with a Canadian named Gary, and where I sit under fans in the heat of the afternoon, before or after work, and drink coffee or tea or cold Coca-Cola, and read for hours or take notes in my field journal.

Today, the regulars are here, as usual: Primo, from Belize, is barefoot on the balcony, with no shirt on, drinking a *cuba libre* (rum and coke) and shouting to someone; Gary is in the corner reading about the Crystal Skulls, and he waves when he sees me, then jumps up to get the chess board; Phil, from England, is at the stove, making a quiche, and teasing the two local women, Marizia and Flora, who are chopping parsley and garlic for garlic butter, shaking knives at him, and dissolving in fits of laughter. Clodagh, Phil's wife, is in the corner with Kayla, a severely-disabled Mayan child with a huge smile who has captured the hearts of all of us. We take turns caring for her and hand feeding her at the restaurant each day.

Dave orders a liter of Gallo Beer, and sits down in his usual spot next to Charlie (remember the guy who passed out in his French toast?). They are a good match, as Charlie is more lost in space than the rest of them. As a 26-year old, his parents pay him to stay out of the United States, because he has caused so much trouble there in North Carolina. Here in San Pedro, he shoots heroine, announces regularly that he is waiting to die, and comes into D'Noz everyday around mid-morning for his first bottle of booze. On good days, Charlie thinks he is Elvis. On bad days he gets thrown out of D'Noz for harassing people and doing lines of cocaine off the bar, or he collapses on the pavement with one of his epileptic seizures. Today he stares silently ahead, drinking a vodka and orange juice (breakfast) while he waits for Dean to get his daily bottle of Cuervo out of the store room.

Since the 1970s, Lake Atitlán has been a refuge for people like Dave and Charlie. There are dozens of people like them in town—a place that was once so difficult to get to that only the most desperate or daring travelers made their way, without roads, through the mountains and around the lake to the Northwest side. Some are simply explorers, traveling through Central America, who have lost their way and chosen to stay. But most are people who have messed up their old lives so badly that they can never go home. They are criminals on the run from the law. From their kids and ex-wives. From reality in general. Lake Atitlán is the kind of place where people change their names and their identities. Where they come to disappear—both body and mind. Rumor has it that even Mick Jagger once passed through San Pedro on a crack binge.

Not all of them are crack-heads and junkies though. There is also a fairly significant contingent of political expatriates. About half of them are from the UK. A quarter of them are Israelis who have fled to Central America in order to avoid their mandatory service in the military (a four-year commitment is required of all Israeli men and women). And the rest are from Germany, Canada, or the States—fleeing right-wing governments and globalization. They are pot-smoking pacifists who, like Clodagh and Phil, spend their free time trying to do good works in the community. When the moon is full, they go to Rainbow Gatherings on the beach.

Once the first restaurant was established and word got out about how easy it was to get drugs in San Pedro, hippies started coming by the dozens. They bought lakefront properties in the lagoon and in San Marcos and established restaurants with vegetarian menus, coffee shops with fresh-baked whole wheat bread and free-trade beans. They built pyramid-shaped yoga retreat centers, holistic massage centers made of bamboo and white linen, and gave hypnotherapy sessions on soft cushions in organic gardens. They created hundreds of jobs for the locals, causing an economic boom that rippled all the way around the lake.

But today the place is changing too fast. You can see it in the dazed look of the *ancianos*. The old Mayan men come into D'Noz wearing *traje* from the neck down, with sunglasses and baseball hats, looking caught halfway between here and there. The old Mayan women seem more trapped than the men—kneeling on the street corners, selling bananas and tomatoes, staring at the tourists with glazed eyes, holding up fingers because they can not tell you the price in Spanish. Only five years ago, they could get away with being monolingual in Tz'utujiil. You can see it in the landscape too: the way cement and tin buildings are smashed in between adobe houses; the way cars and buses rumble through the cobblestone streets not built for so much traffic; the way the chickens and dogs pick through the piles of plastic trash that blanket the ground under the coffee trees; the way children will not dress or talk like their grandparents anymore because to get jobs in the capital they have to hide their Maya-ness.

The town is just like the two tectonic plates crashing together underneath it. It is a fault line, where the old ways and the new ways are grinding against each other. Causing uplift. And upheaval. And if the time comes when the looks deep inside people's faces say they don't really want us here, would we listen? Would the earth start trembling, too?

Watching Clodagh rock Kayla in her arms on the couch in D'Noz, I decide that not all change is bad change.

Perhaps with caring people passing through town, and making an effort, children like Kayla will know that they are loved, even if they cannot work to feed their families and are abused and shunned and treated like garbage.

I walk over to them and sit down on the coffee table. "How's she doing today?" I ask, slipping my finger into the girl's tiny fist.

Kayla's head rolls back, unsupported by her neck, and a huge smile consumes her face. Her mouth opens wide, and I can see down into her throat as a soft laugh shakes her body, exposing a tiny purple uvula. Her sunken brown eyes glisten with permanent tears, as she stares up at the restaurant's exposed ceiling beams.

"Did you hear that? I've never heard her laugh before," Clodagh says, stroking her black hair. "She likes you."

The same thing that cracked inside me when Leslie put her head on my shoulder during the weaving lesson, cracks again when I am with Kayla. She splits me open down the middle.

Here is Kayla's story: Her parents are alive and healthy, and have three healthy children, but Kayla is a burden and they ignore her most of the time, waiting for her to die. Phil and Clodagh, found Kayla one evening when they heard her screaming. They broke down the door of the room where she was lying, tied to the bed, looking as though she had been left there for days. "In a puddle of her own vomit and urine," Phil tells me. "She was on the verge of death."

They rushed her to the doctor, where she was put on an IV and re-hydrated. The best he could tell them was that Kayla had never recovered from a near-fatal case of meningitis she'd had as a two-year old. The disease had damaged her brain and left her muscles atrophied, stunting her growth. Being carried around in a sling on her mother's back for years because she couldn't walk had folded up her limbs like a pretzel. Trying to move them at all to exercise them made her cringe. The doctor estimated that she was probably about eight years old now, but also said she could probably make a partial recovery with therapy, learn to speak, and maybe walk again.

Phil and Clodagh took her to their friend, Felipe's house up the hill, where she was fed and bathed, and her clothes washed. Felipe, a *Pedrano* who owns a local *comedor* and has a family of his own, kept her until Kayla's family accused him of kidnapping and demanded she be returned.

"Why?" I ask Phil. "It didn't seem like they wanted her before. Why did they want her now that someone was actually taking care of her?"

"Felipe actually offered to adopt her," Phil says. "But in this community, it is more embarrassing to have a child taken away to be raised by someone else, than to have it die from disease. So they just hide her away in a back room and forget about her for days on end. They are ashamed of her. She is an extra mouth to feed and she can't contribute back anything to the family. She can't weave. Can't learn to cook. She's just a burden to them—at least in their perspective."

Because the family would no longer let Felipe see Kayla after he gave her back, Phil and Clodagh offered to start taking her during the day for just a few days a week, convincing her parents that they weren't actually kidnapping her, but just taking her to a special school, a small clinic set up for the disabled, where she would be cared for all day, and have contact with other children. At the end of the afternoon on Tuesdays and Thursdays, they take her for a bath and massage at Solar Pools (a tourist place run by a Canadian couple with private solar-heated tubs in a garden) and bring her to D'Noz, where Dean feeds her for free, cooking soft, enriching foods, like scrambled eggs and guacamole.

That afternoon, while I play chess with Gary, people come and go constantly, bartering and trading with Dean, bringing old Rum jugs full of juice and borrowing cucumbers or limes. Kayla is the center of attention, and crowds gather around her, cooing and asking how she is doing. She smiles and squeals when people touch her face, lets her head roll around, and doesn't resist as much as usual while Clodagh works on her muscles, gently exercising her arms and legs.

Later, I walk Kayla home with Phil, hoping to meet her parents and speak with them. Neither Clodagh or Phil speak very good Spanish, and they have asked for my help in attempting to break through to her parents' soft sides. Along the way, we sidestep piles of green horse manure and the back of my neck prickles with sweat. I swat continuously at the gnats landing near Kayla's eyes and mouth.

We turn off the road into a yard adjacent to an abandoned café. Beside it stands a corrugated tin and wood-slat shack. The door is locked with a padlock.

"It's nice to see they're eager for their daughter to come home," Phil says, pointing to the lock. "I swear. Sometimes it's like they can't even be bothered to remember she exists at all. I've gotta get to work. Do you mind waiting with her?"

"Of course not." I take her from him, and sit down on the step, her body resting so tiny and breakable in my arms. Her muscles are so stiff that every time I shift, I am afraid of hurting her. Her skin hangs loosely off her bones, and her limbs stay frozen and she grinds her teeth, until after half an hour, she finally relaxes and falls asleep.

The yard around us is littered with soiled diapers, food remains, and broken plastic buckets. Textiles and white sheets hang on a clothesline draped between two avocado trees. Half a dozen chickens wander around pecking at the dirt.

"What are you doing with Kayla?" a voice barks, out of nowhere.

Kayla jerks awake and starts moaning and grinding her teeth again.

The woman huffs and pulls Kayla from my arms, and takes her through an iron gate to a windowless room, depositing her on a bed. Before I can gather my senses and register what has happened, the woman locks the gate, and disappears around the corner, without giving me a second glance. I watch Kayla through the bars, writhing with discomfort on the bed, and there is nothing I can do.

I don't scream when I see the shadow on my hotel room wall, flickering in the light of my candle, but I want to. I walk outside calmly and find Pedro in the *tienda*.

"Can you help me?" I say, blushing. "There's a scorpion in my room."

He smiles. "Ah, but scorpions are a sign of positive change and fertility," he says coming around with a broom. "One time I got stung," he says, opening the gate. "Right here, putting my finger on the latch. It was dark and I didn't see it, and Ayyyy!" he demonstrates, jerking his finger back and shaking his arm in the air.

"Did it hurt bad?" I ask.

"Oh, *sí*. For about four hours I wanted to cut off my whole arm. But it gets better pretty quickly with the black ones. The worst are the *alacranes*. Red scorpions. Smaller. But *ay*. You don't want to get stung by one of those."

"What happens then?"

"You need *antibioticos*, or you might die."

I add *alacránes* to the list of things that might kill me in Guatemala.

The scorpion in my room is a big black one, not an *alacrán*, but Pedro sweeps it outside into the garden and steps on the tail anyway. "They travel in pairs," he says, chuckling. "So, watch out for the other one."

"Thanks," I say.

Of course, after that, I can't sleep. I thrash around in my bed, lifting the sheets every so often and checking with a flashlight for more scorpions. There have been a number of stories about them floating around at D'Noz: A scorpion molting on a pillow, leaving its shell in perfect scorpion shape as a gift to Primo, right next to his face; a sandbag left under a bed where a scorpion decided to lay eggs. Undetected, the bag became filled with scorpions over the course of a few months until Monica finally found it. She turned the squirming bundle over to her landlord who drenched the sack with gasoline and incinerated it.

Visions of squirming, flaming scorpions peck at me each time I drift into sleep, repeatedly jerking me awake. I think about Kayla.

I sat in that yard and waited for her parents until after dark when the full moon was up, shining over the lake. I sat there listening to Kayla cry inside that room, unable to help her, while packs of dogs came growling and barking through the yard, chasing around bitches in heat, and drunk men passed by shouting and falling down in the street. I sat there until her parents finally came home after 10 p.m. And by then, I was too exhausted to say what I had waited so long to say, and I just introduced myself and asked if I could come back and see Kayla in the morning.

As I lay sleepless in bed, I think about kidnapping her. About smuggling her across the border in Mexico, through the desert, putting her in a suitcase if I have to. She is small enough, after all. I think of anything that could get her to a place where people will care for her.

I think about how it might be better if she were with my parents back in Baltimore. They raised two adopted children from El Salvador and I think of how gentle they would be with her, after having so much patience with my adopted brother and sister. I think about taking her myself. Changing everything. How much better her life could be, instead of cursed to live in San Pedro, locked in a room, unable to even pull her own pants down when she needs to go to the bathroom, unable to speak her pain or hunger in words, isolated from kindness and human contact. From a tender touch. From love.

I think about how she relaxed and smiled when I

brushed my fingers softly across her face and hair. I think about breaking down that door and kidnapping her or putting her out of her misery. I think about suffocating her with a pillow.

As it turns out, the scorpion *was* a positive sign. A few days later, after a good degree of persistence, I am making some progress with Kayla's parents. In fact, Reuben and Ana seem to be such meek people—good people—who find it easier to cope with their situation by pretending she doesn't exist. One day, they take me into their home and show me pictures of Kayla as a healthy baby, with tears welling up in their eyes. It seems they have been so dull to pain for so long—getting no compassion from the community for their daughter—and now suddenly with me pushing them to reconcile their grief and to cry their tears, they are starting to see. I fall into the role of therapist, and it's okay.

The town is too poor to spend effort and money on children who will never grow up to help their families. Reuben and Ana wear their hardened-stone hearts on their faces, but looking at both of them, I see them aching to crumble. They are just people like me, who desperately need someone to talk to, to help them feel their pain, to help them confront it and to move on and open up to their daughter, because no one is really going to kidnap her or suffocate her with a pillow to put her out of her misery, and she needs them.

Reuben tells me he only makes 10 or 12 quetzales a day working for the coffee *beneficio,* loading and unloading dripping wet sacks of beans and raking them out on the barbeque. He has three other children to feed. And he has Kayla. He is trying to save money for his wife Ana, so she can get an orange juice stand.

Shortly after I start spending time with them, and with Kayla, Reuben gets a second job at Solar Pools as a gardener, and Ana buys an orange press, and a glass case so that she can sell sliced watermelon, pineapple, and homemade donuts to the tourists. The more time I spend talking with them, the more they start letting Kayla sit outside, in her wheelchair, though they still cover her with a veil, to keep her hidden. But sometimes they leave her alone out there for hours, while they work, and they tie her to the chair so she won't fall out. I can't pass by the house without thinking of her, and most of the time I stop in to visit. Kayla becomes the most important part of my routine. She is the only part of my anthropological journey that seems to matter at all, so far. When I am with her, I feel like I am actually making a difference in one life, like I have a purpose for being here, in this crazy land of drugs, culture clash, contradiction, and fear.

SPIRIT WORLD

I hear mornings in San Pedro long before I awake to them: A generator puttering on the hillside. The crowing of roosters. The pounding of hammers against cinder block, alternating with the thump of a man's axe as he splits wood, and the clapping back and forth of a woman's hands, as corn tortillas take shape between them. The music of Atitlán is constant, and it has crescendos and decrescendos, accented notes and fermatas, just like any other symphony, rising and falling, the rhythm changing with the time of day—the melody echoing the moods of the rain and wind and moon and sun.

Most days, when I am not at D'Noz or with Kayla, I sit out on the rocks and meditate, do yoga stretches in the garden, light candles and incense in my room, and steam vegetables and wild rice. I sometimes invite Pedro's kids into my room and we watch DVDs in Spanish on my laptop (I bought dubbed versions of *Shrek* and *Aladdin* from the Blockbuster in Guate), and they pick up my cameras and pens and notebooks and my mouse pad and say, "Can I have this?" over and over again. And I give them crayons and paper, and they sprawl out on the floor and draw pictures.

Sometimes I take long walks around town and up to

the market with my camera and notebook, documenting everything in my field journal. I write about the children who play basketball in the court next to the church, and the pick-up trucks that sit in the road with their beds full of used American clothing—everything for one Quetzal. I document the words painted on walls all over down. *Jesús es tu única esperanza. Busca a Diós. Jesús es Señor de San Pedro.* Jesus is your only hope. Look for God. Jesus is Lord of San Pedro. I find a picture of the town painted five years earlier and photograph it. Then I go to that spot and take a picture at the same place (Fig 2 and 3). I sit on the steps outside the market with books in Tz'utujiil and Spanish that I've gotten from the library of the *Academia Maya*, and I try to read the Tz'utujiil aloud, butchering the pronunciation and making all the kids gathered around me roll and clutch their bellies with laughter. They try to coach me, unsuccessfully, to say it right.

I sit in town for hours and hours and watch things happen, with my field journal on my knee and my camera around my neck. I write about gender division, and how all the men in the market deal with the animal products—the meat, the leather, the cheap trinkets and trade goods off the trucks from Guatemala City. Women sell fruit and vegetables, and bowls and pots and things for the home. I write about how the air in the center smells like rancid chicken because there is no refrigeration and flies land on everything. I write about how one day, ordering my ground beef in the market I see blood dripping from intestines hanging on a hook, and I throw up on the floor. Shortly after that a man carrying a headless cow carcass on his back bumps into me.

I become a vegetarian.

No chicken, no fish, no meat at all. Just eggs and cheese and beans and a lot of fruits and vegetables. And rice. And tea. Lots of tea. I become obsessed with making infusions from the herbs I buy in San Marcos after my yoga classes. They are grown with "loving-kindness." They are Buddhist herbs. I make dozens of infusions from them, combining lemongrass and lavender when I have a headache, or boiling oregano for fifteen minutes for menstrual cramps, or adding honey to an herb called *Orozus* when I have a sore throat to fight off a cold, or making an *Epizote* when I get amoebas from the lake water.

I feel like a medicine woman.

But it is nothing compared to the knowledge of the Maya. They have *atoles* and *remedias* for everything, and when I come down with a chest cough that lasts for weeks, I track down a shaman who tells me to squeeze an orange from a certain tree, mince some sweet onion, leave the mixture overnight and drink a glass of it three times the next day. "Your cough will be gone," he says, throwing his hands up in the air. "Like *brujería*." Like witchcraft. I try his remedy, and it is bitingly sour and has a chunky texture that is hard to swallow. It seems to help a little. But with all the dust in the air, the dryness is deep inside everyone's chests and we are all coughing, praying for rain.

It takes a few months of being in San Pedro for me to get a sense for how much shamanism and witchcraft is practiced there. When Dean breaks his ribs, he ices them for weeks but they never get better. Then one day I come into D'Noz and see a man lighting candles while his wife adjusts pillows then holds Dean's arms back. The man is a *curandero de huesos,* a bonesetter, a revered position in Tz'utujiil society.

Once everyone is in position, he says some sacred verses in Tz'utujiil and starts whacking and thrusting in on Dean's ribcage. Dean yelps with pain, but the bonesetter doesn't stop. Tears squeeze out of Dean's eyes and he struggles to get away. I start to wonder if I should intervene and make it stop. Finally the bonesetter is satisfied, and rubs oil on Dean's chest and abdomen. He collects his fee of 30 Quetzales and says goodbye.

"Did it help?" I ask him, after the bonesetter has left and Dean has chugged half a bottle of Jack Daniels.

"Lord, no," he says breathing heavily, hunched over in pain.

The next morning though, he shows me his chest and the bruises are miraculously diminished. "Yesterday I thought that guy was a total, bloody quack," he says. "But today I feel better than I have in days." His ribs heal completely within a week.

It seems like just about everyone in San Pedro believes in some kind of magic. Among hippies it is all reincarnation, crystals, chakras, and auras. Among the Tz'utujiiles, it is more shamans and witches, and sweats, and respect for certain gods, and different colored candles that do different things. In one interview, I learn that for the Maya, the hours of twelve noon and midnight are bewitched hours. They are times during which you are not supposed to work. Times when the *characoteles* and *brujos* (witches and sorcerers) do their work. It is important to stay in the house during this time. Quietly. Respectfully. If you ignore this, bad things happen.

I am told of a pregnant woman who lost track of time and found herself at the lakeshore washing clothes on the rocks at noon. She suddenly felt a pain in her stomach, and heard the cry of a baby. But she looked around and could not find a baby. She went home and became sick and soon found out that she was no longer pregnant. Her husband raced back down to the lakeshore to look for the child but could not find it, though he swears he could also hear it screaming. When he got home, his wife was dead.

Since then, others claim to have heard the sound of a child screaming at the rocks, and some say they have even seen a baby crawling into a cave. According to the woman who told me this story, even a Canadian tourist claims to have seen the child and heard it crying.

I also interview an *anciano* who tells me a story about how as a young child he was walking in the fields one day and saw an animal—something like a rabbit, but he wasn't sure—hopping away. He wanted to catch the animal and take it home with him, so he chased it, and suddenly he found himself sitting in the kitchen of a woman who lived on the other side of town. At seeing him, she knew instantly that he was possessed and she came after him with a broom. An instant later he found himself back in the field, it was nighttime and the stars were shining.

He went home and found that three days had passed, and that his family had searched through the hills and fields and found no trace of him. Also, he could no longer speak. The experience had rendered him mute. The family consulted a shaman, who returned to the field where they boy had disappeared and performed a ceremony with candles and incense, with the boy asking forgiveness for his disrespect. After the ceremony, he was able to speak again.

While these stories are interesting and absurd, they don't seem to be getting me anywhere. I keep trying to get people to talk about the violence of the 1980s, thinking that is the essential crisis that has these people reeling. I gently ask them to remember their family members who died, and to tell me what had happened, and they do willingly for a few minutes. But no matter what I bring up in my interviews, the subject always turns to hoaky spirits, the tourists and their drugs, and to strange things that happen here if you are paying attention. They talk about ghosts. Haunted winds. Spirits of ancestors. Of sacred islands that sank into the lake, taking chests of treasure with them. Of ancient cities buried in the mountains. Of places where you can walk across abandon pit houses and feel that the ground is hollow under your feet. Of an ancient tunnel that stretches from Quetzaltenango to the temples of Tikal, clear on the other side of Guatemala. Of enchanted caves in the mountains where the Tz'utujiiles hid when Pedro de Alvarado came.

The more stories I hear, the more my mind tries to open to them. I come to my interviews feeling more and more like an anthropologist. When I leave the interview room, I slowly start taking elements of the stories with me. They are told with such conviction, such belief, that I have trouble not believing that there are unseen forces at work in San Pedro. I start to feel shifts in the town's energy. I start to notice how the dogs go crazy during the full moon. I start to feel like I am truly communing with the earth during my meditations. Like Tarot cards are actually speaking to me, and birds landing on nearby branches and gusts of wind are signs of my connectivity. Like I am tapping in. But being an atheist and a blank slate should mean that there is nothing else, just science, just nature. So how can I explain the surges of energy? Sometimes I think they come from within me, especially when streetlights and transformers blow out right over my head as I pass by. There is a raw connection to the deep and mystical nature of this place that I can't justify unless there is something spiritual or energetic at work.

By the end of May, I am counting down the days to a welcome, extended visit from Elena, who is arriving mid-June for an open-ended backpacking trip with me, starting in Antigua. It will be a little vacation from my fieldwork, and San Pedro is strange enough that I am ready for a break. Best of all, Elena was raised as an atheist, and I'm ready to pick her brain.

People all over town are lighting candles for rain. The clouds come in heavier every afternoon, sending ripples of thunder through the sky, making the place feel so full of energy that the lightning bolts on the volcano are like the unleashing of the earth itself. God or no god, there is no doubt about it, San Pedro is alive and breathing. It is a place where the land doesn't keep secrets. It just comes right out and says what it means, and people listen.

And then it finally happens. One afternoon, the heat grows heavy and humid, and the clouds turn a dark, even gray and rain comes down straight and warm, pouring in sheets. The volcanoes hide behind the clouds. Thunder rumbles, the electricity goes out, and people come and stand in their doorways, just watching the torrents cascade over the tin roofs and wash through the streets. Pathways become rivers that flow into the lake.

I sit out in it, letting it drench me, and watch the drops hitting the stalks of grass, pelting the surface of the lake and pounding against tin roofs, making all the leaves and flower petals dance, soaking into the earth. Workers run back from the fields, some holding burlap sacks over their heads, others just strolling home with their faces to the sky, letting the rain drench them. I open my mouth and feel the drops pelt my face. I let it splash up dirty from the ground, splattering onto my feet and legs.

When the rain stops, the birds go crazy. They dart all over the place, chirping and singing and ruffling their feathers. Children run around, giggling and covered with mud, and wet and laughing and playing. The air is rich, wet, warm, loamy, the sweet way only volcanic soil can smell. Leftover raindrops fall from tree branches and from roofs. As evening comes, candles burn in all the houses, and the songs of tree frogs and crickets and the scent of night-blooming jasmine fill the air.

San Pedro is crisp and clean. The dust settles, and in the air there is a sense of release. The rainy season has begun.

THE CLIMB

When you take the earth, in its purest, most secular form, volcanoes are the birthplaces of everything. They are at once like great motherly breasts, swelling high and huge with the hot milk of the earth, and like burning wombs, exploding into the sky, showering down a new beginning, covering the countryside with a fresh layer of ash and fertile soil.

They are the essence of motherliness, comforting presences on the horizon, inviting us with their softness to linger around them, to photograph them, climb them, and press our faces to the ground, just as we once pressed them against our own mothers' breasts. In Guatemala, when the earth is stirring, the red glow in the night and the thick plumes of smoke spiraling upwards into the morning sky are a reminder that the planet is alive and restless, and throbbing with energy. Those who live here, along the volcanic cordillera, have witnessed the flowing, burning, 4,000-degree blood of the earth, and are conscious of its rhythm and power, conducting their lives in time with the pulsating heartbeat of the planet itself.

The string of active volcanoes in Guatemala are called "Strato" volcanoes. They are the kind with perfect triangular cones that belch out flaming rocks, and sometimes spew black smoke and ash 10 kilometers into the sky, flowering over the land in colossal mushroom clouds that tinge sunsets for weeks. The lava is more viscous than a'a, and is often about 50 percent rock, which can act as a plug, causing massive eruptions, like the one thousands of years ago that formed the 26-kilometer crater that is now the breathtaking *caldera* of Lake Atitlán.

June 14, 2002

It is just past noon, and thunderheads are building up around the volcanoes, when Elena arrives from the States to join me for an extended backpacking trip through Guatemala and the Yucatan Peninsula. After bobbing her way through the airport crowd and throwing her skinny arms around my neck, she looks out at the cordillera of darkened volcanoes from where we wait for a taxi to Antigua, points in awe, and says in a hushed voice, "We have to climb one of those."

"Okay," I say, leaning up against her, breathing in her smoky, evergreen scent, relishing the first physical closeness I've had in months. "But we might get robbed by bandits." This is a real concern on Volcán Pacaya, and there have been some horrific crimes committed. It is recommended to hire an armed guide, to deter thieves who have been known to brutally attack, and even rape and murder tourists on their climb.

"Oooh, bandits," she says, opening her eyes wide and giggling.

I love Elena for a lot of reasons, but right now I love her most because she is fearless and crazy. As soon as I see the glint in her eyes, I understand how much I have let the fear get to me. Now that I have her as a companion, I won't have to think about the emptiness that God left behind, because she will fill it. We can push the boundaries together. We can go out at night, flirt with guys, travel to new places, jump off of cliffs into swimming holes, skinny-dip, and climb volcanoes.

In the taxi on the way to Antigua, I try to explain my deviation from religion to Elena, who is a life-long atheist, but also majored in anthropology at Franklin and Marshall College, like me. I respect her intelligence and her thinking. "What do you think happens when we die?" I ask her.

She shrugs. "We go into the ground."

Volcán Pacaya, south of Esquintla and Guatemala City, has been in its current active phase since 1965, with activity ranging from steam columns and strombolian light shows to huge explosions. In September 1998, an eruption showered three feet of ash down onto the runways of the airport in Guate, forcing it to close. In January 2000, Pacaya erupted again, with reports of lava flows on the south slope. Satellite imagery indicated that an ash cloud rose to 25,000 feet above sea level. A year later, a seismometer recorded over 700 earthquakes per day, with sulfur gas emissions elevating the volcano again to a state of red alert.

Beside Pacaya, the Agua, Fuego, and Acatenango volcanoes rise to more than 12,000 feet. Dwarfed in comparison to her taller triangular neighbors, Pacaya looks gentle, round, and unimposing. At a mere 8,373 feet, she sits in their shadow, and cannot be seen from the valley two hours away, where the guided tours start out in Antigua. With a steam vent that provides electricity to six departments, a lake of clear potable water, and terraced agricultural fields of rich black soil, Pacaya is considered less of a threat, and more of a giver of life.

In the year 2001, the land above the town of San Francisco de Sales was set aside as "Pacaya National Park," and a rigorous effort was made to eliminate the bandits. Prior to the establishment of the park, when climbing Pacaya, educated travelers hit the scree slopes fully expecting to be robbed. To many of them, it was part of the adventure. They paid children in the village of San Francisco de Sales to watch their vehicles, and left their watches, their passports, their wallets behind in their hotel rooms, carrying only enough cash to appease the thieves. Sometimes the bandits stopped them right at the trailhead and demanded visitors pay a "toll" to climb the mountain.

Despite the designation as a National Park, there are still few safety precautions taken at the summit. Most climbers hike right up to the edge of the crater and crane their necks over the edge, hoping to see lava. Occasionally, they are injured as showers of sizzling rocks spew from the mouth of the volcano. There are endless stories of tourists and guides running for their lives down the mountain, even deaths. I tell Elena all of this on the night before our climb, as we drink Gallo beer and play pool at Frida's Bar in Antigua.

She shrugs, swats at the eight-ball, and says, "I'd rather die living than live dying."

The next morning, like many in the rainy season, is deceptively cheerful. There is a rosy sunrise, a slight breeze, and volcanoes against a blue sky. Elena and I eat huge, protein-rich breakfasts, pack extra bottled water, bright yellow ponchos and a change of clothes (because despite the serenity of morning, we know we'll probably get caught in the rain), granola bars, and flashlights. The trip doesn't leave until afternoon, and from other climbers we've heard that we'll be coming down in the dark. "We're totally prepared," I say to Elena. "No surprises."

"Oh man," she says, pouting playfully. "That's no fun."

I slide 200 Quetzales and a photocopy copy of my passport into my back pocket, like I always do before trips like this. As an afterthought, I include my Fulbright ID badge, and leave my cell phone in the hotel room, figuring it will be useless all the way out on Pacaya—just something more for the bandits to steal. We are giggling and giddy, and we skip down the street towards the corner where we will meet the bus, arriving just before 1 p.m. to find a dozen other tourists leaning against the wall, patiently waiting with no bus in sight. It is obvious by their lack of concern that they have been in Central America long enough to understand how transportation here works.

But by 1:30 we are still waiting, and a few people start to wonder anyone is coming to get us. "We're not going to even make it to the park until three," someone says. "And that's if they show up right now."

Talking with the others, we learn that most of them are just passing through Guatemala on their Central America circuit. One couple, Paul Brace and Lisa Jury, are engaged, and they are here on a pre-wedding honeymoon. It is Paul's first journey outside of Canada. "He's so proud of that stamp on his passport," Lisa says, smiling and squeezing his hand.

At 2:15, a white van finally pulls up and a man introduces himself as Alejandro and collects our reservation slips. It is 2:45 before we are on the road towards Esquintla, and dark clouds are already building over the volcanoes. We drive south past Guatemala City, and the air grows heavy and cool, moisture settling on our skin through the open window. We wind around curves, as clouds fill the sky, and we roar up hills past pick-up trucks loaded with *campesinos* in traditional Mayan dress. They stare at us—at our van that says *TURISMO* in big black letters on the side, at our cameras and baseball hats, at our shiny Gore-Tex jackets, and Nalgene bottles dangling from purple karabiners.

Each time we fling around a curve, some people gasp and grab at the seats, and some people giggle nervously. I am laughing and relaxed, because I have gotten used to these rides by now, and I lean back and forth with the curves, teasing Elena. Beside me, she is bouncing around in her seat, clapping her hands like a child.

"This is great!" she squeals when the van comes up on two wheels during a turn. "I *love* Guatemala."

At 3:30, the sky darkening with clouds, we turn onto

the dirt road that leads up the mountain to San Francisco de Sales, and as we bounce over ruts and rocks, the electricity in the van reaches a fever pitch. "I want to see lava," Paul says, grabbing Lisa's hand. "Do you think we will?"

Just after 5:00 p.m., Elena and I come wheezing out of the woods after a steep 2-mile climb, emerging onto a treeless ridge cloaked with swirling clouds. They clear intermittently, to give us fleeting glimpses of the cinder cone towering overhead. The ground beneath our feet is black, gravelly and crunches under our feet. The sky gets heavier and heavier on our skin with each passing minute.

We rest with the group at the rim of a dried lava flow and a wooden sign that says "stay away from the edge." Despite the weather, Elena is her usual self, bouncing around and talking to everyone, with beads of dew collecting on her black hair and eyelashes. For fun, we take close-up pictures of each other, trying to capture the dew and the essence of the moment. We lend our cameras to Lisa, and she takes one of us leaning together, and we take some of her and Paul.

I watch him wrap an arm around Lisa's waist as they embrace for the camera. After the picture, he looks at her and sweeps a strand of hair out of her face, tucking it sweetly behind her ear. "You okay?" he asks.

She nods and kisses him. He takes her hand and they hike in front of us, Paul slowing his stride to match her rhythm.

The cone looms above us. The ground sloping away from the trail is covered with sculptures, designs, and words made from lava chunks and rock. It is reminiscent of a high school bathroom stall, only without the profanity, and I have an urge to climb down and write "Cindy wuz here." We hike along the edge of the lava fields, and finally arrive at the south slope, where a line of dark, silhouetted hikers are climbing single file up the 45-

degree slope, disappearing into the clouds.

Elena and Paul are very strong climbers, and soon they are way ahead of the group. I am the last to join the procession, and I leave Lisa, and two Dutch women, named Annette and Tamara behind, sitting on a boulder, because they are tired and want to rest at the cone's base. They say they don't need to make the final climb. It is okay with them if they don't reach the summit or see lava. I myself would like to stop here, but I decide to go for it, knowing it will be hard to listen to Elena talk about all the wonderful sights from the top if I don't make it up there.

It is the most physically challenging experience of my life so far. As my boots plunge into the cinder surface, it gives way beneath them, sending a shower of sand and ash down behind me, so that every few minutes I have to stop to let the rockslide subside and to catch my balance. For each step forward I slide two back. My calves burn, but I push on. I stumble constantly, my legs wobbling like water. I can feel the altitude pushing on my chest, making my breath come shallow and fast.

About half way up, I collapse on the slope, rest, and eat a handful of nuts for energy. On a flat spot above me, Paul waves and shouts something into the wind. He has a huge smile on his face, and I'm not sure what he's yelling, but what I think I hear is, *You're almost there! You can do it!* I pull myself up and push on, only taking ten more steps before I have to rest again. Climbing this scree slope is like scrambling up a sand dune in an earthquake. I take ten more steps and rest. Then ten more, and rest. And somehow I make it up Pacaya, ten steps at a time.

Just before I reach the summit, the rain begins in a quick burst. I have barely enough time to pull my poncho out of my bag before I am completely soaked. The din of it on the plastic hood is loud and rhythmic, and water pours over my face, and down my legs into my shoes.

When I finally make those last ten steps, Paul slaps me on the shoulder and congratulates me. "Great job!" he says. "I knew you could do it."

"Did you see lava?" I say.

"No, too many clouds and a lot of smoke. But it is still really cool. There's a lot of yellow and green, and you can look right down into the crater." He points me towards the crater, then heads off on his own to explore, walking around the south slope.

As I follow the narrow path around, the sky opens up completely and drilling torrents pelt down on my head. The wind whips past me, and sheets of horizontal rain slam against my poncho, which inflates like a sail. I hunker down, hoping I don't get blown over the edge. I walk past a man crouched under an umbrella, trying to find shelter beside a boulder. He has scooped one of the stray dogs in his arms, and shoves it under the folds of his trench coat.

I see the rest of our group huddled at the crater's edge and I walk towards them. At that moment, the wind swirls around, and a cloud of sulfur dioxide smoke envelops them. The volcanic gas is dangerous to inhale, because it can combine with water in their lungs and become sulfuric acid, which burns terribly. They come towards me at a full sprint, emerging from the yellow cloud coughing and holding their hands over their chests.

Elena tugs at my arm as she goes past. "Come on, Cindy," she shouts over the roar of the rain. "We have to go down."

"I'll be right behind you. I'm so close. I just want to see the crater." I pull away from her and move towards it.

"You can't even see anything," she shouts after me. "There's too much gas. We have to go, now!"

I glance longingly towards the crater, then turn to follow her. Everyone is rushing past with their clothes so wet that their shirts are clinging to their ribs and bellies. Some of them are still coughing. Others hold their collars up over their noses, and the rain streams over their faces. The noise of the rain is deafening.

Then, there is a crack so loud that I scream and throw

my hands over my ears. Then another crack. And a blast of light. I scream again, and fall to my knees. *I've died,* I think. *I'm dead.*

But after a few seconds, I begin to feel the jagged shards of volcanic rock digging into my calves, and my senses slowly return. I feel the prickle of the hairs on my arms, reaching toward my poncho. The air around me sizzles with electricity. My nose burns with the smell of ozone and sulfur. My eyes open and I squint through a blur of raindrops and see everyone running frantically past me, with their hair puffed out under their hoods. They speak to me, waving their arms, but I can't hear them over the pounding rain. But I do hear the third rumble of thunder. My body moves as if some deep primordial instinct has been triggered. I have one clear thought: *Down. I must get down.*

I fly down off the slope, skiing the rocks and ash without thinking, as if I am an Olympic, volcano-skiing champion. I don't worry about falling. I just ride on the back of the landslide that is tumbling down under me, resting my weight back on my heels. Scree gathers in my shoes under my arches, scraping away at my skin, but I don't really notice. There isn't time.

As I approach the cone's base seconds later, where the group is gathered, a thin, frail figure waits apart from the others. It is Lisa, shivering under a nylon pack cover which she holds over her head. She yells something to me, but I can't hear. She yells again.

"Is Paul behind you?" She is drenched, her clothes sucking close to her skin. She looks smaller than before.

"I don't think so. I'm the last one down." I peer at the huddle of people gathered around the boulders where we left Lisa, Annette, and Tamara. There aren't quite enough of them. "Where's the rest of the group?" I ask.

"Some of them ran right past me and just kept going down to the bottom. Are you sure Paul's not still up there?"

I shake my head. "I definitely didn't see anyone else up there," I say. "Maybe he got past you somehow in the confusion and went down to the bottom with the others?"

"No," she says, looking up at the cone again. "He would have waited for me."

"Let's go talk to our guide. He has a radio and can check with the station to see if he's down below."

Lisa is trembling.

"I'm sure Paul's fine," I say. "We'll find him. Don't worry."

She shakes her head. "No. Something's happened. Something's wrong."

When Lisa starts to wobble, Tamara moves in quickly, supporting her. Our guide, Augusto, tries to radio down to the guard station to see if he can find Paul there, but no one seems to know how many people we had in our group to begin with, so our count means very little. Additionally, there are other tour groups who have gotten mixed in with ours. I imagine the scene of chaos at the park entrance, where the other guides are trying to count everyone. Radio messages are garbled incoherent shouts. "Twenty four. We have twenty four. Three from *Grupo Jaguar*. Twenty six. Seven from *Barco*. Four Jaguar."

Augusto finally gives up on the radio and decides to go back up the cone and look for Paul. He leaves us huddled together in the rain while he climbs back up to the summit. We wait and wait.

By 7:30 it is almost completely dark. I sit down on a rock and dump the debris out of my shoes. The scree has worn holes through the bottoms of my SmartWool socks. Withered white blisters peel off the soles of my feet, but it is so wet that there is no pain, just dead skin.

"Maybe we should get moving," Elena says, pointing to Lisa who is starting to shiver more violently. "It's getting pretty cold and dark."

I shove my shredded socks in my bag and put my shoes back on without them. I look up to see that everyone is watching me. Waiting. Apparently, I am supposed to make a decision about what we do next. They seem to think I will have answers, perhaps because I have been translating from Spanish all day, and they know that I have been in Guatemala for six months now. In their eyes, it makes me the expert.

A twinge of resentfulness slips through my mind. *I just want to go back to Antigua and take a shower and eat some dinner.* But I ignore it because we came as a group, and we can't leave until we find him. "Right," I say, finally, accepting this strange call to duty. "We have to go down, now."

"But shouldn't we wait for Augusto?" Lisa says, still trembling.

"No," Tamara says. "We're wasting time here. We should be looking for Paul. He could be on the trail with a broken leg, getting hypothermic or something."

"He didn't come past me. I swear," Lisa says.

"The fact is that it's getting dark," I say. "We're all soaked. These are the perfect conditions for hypothermia, and we really do need to get off the mountain now and find some shelter. Otherwise we're going *all* going to get hypothermic, and we'll have nine missing people instead of just one." I look around and people in the circle are nodding. "Okay then," I say. "Let's all stick together and we'll use our lights to look for him and call his name as we go down. Augusto can find us at the bottom. Is everybody ready?"

The rain slows and the crickets begin to chirp in the meadow. We set off at a light jog towards the tree line in the distance, calling Paul's name, with the beams from our flashlights cutting through the fog.

THE SEARCH

"Paul!" I shout. The light wobbles in front of me into the trees, cutting through the darkness, bouncing off branches, and disappearing into the foliage. There is the sound of breathing and footsteps, and water dripping from the canopy.

"PAUL!" someone else shouts. "Paul are you out there?"

We run with our eyes darting from the tangled mess of roots under our feet to the underbrush of the forest, searching for some sign that he has come this way. A torn piece of clothing. Maybe one of his yellow gloves hanging from a tree branch. Maybe we have seen too many movies. We find nothing.

Twenty minutes and two miles later, we arrive breathless at the park entrance. The place is deserted, except for a few members of our group who are milling around in the parking lot, looking impatiently at their watches. A handful of children run up to us, selling cold sodas that we buy and chug greedily, without stopping for air.

At the guard shack, I speak to the park rangers.

"He probably just got lost in the rain," one of them says, tossing his hands.

"He might have wandered down the wrong side of the volcano," says another. "So he'll probably end up in one of the villages and take a chicken bus back to Antigua. That's what usually happens."

"Usually?" I say. "How often does this kind of thing happen?"

He shrugs. "*De vez en cuando.*" From time to time.

But both hypotheses seem unlikely to me. Lisa says that Paul is more knowledgeable in the outdoors than anyone she has ever known. If anyone would know what to do in an emergency, it's him. He grew up with the Canadian Rockies in his backyard. She says it over and over again. He would have waited for her. *Something is wrong.* I try to picture him slashing through brush on the wrong side of the volcano, popping out onto a highway in the middle of the night and wandering along the roadside, looking for a ride. But that scenario seems ridiculous. "Is there a radio?" I ask. "Maybe we can call someone in these villages and ask them to keep an eye out for him. Just so we'll know he's okay?"

"No, *señorita. No hay radio.* Just walkie talkies."

I sigh. This is getting nowhere. "What kind of emergency are we really looking at here?" I ask. "What's the worst that could have happened to him?"

"He could have fallen into the crater," one of the guards says casually. "If that happened, we'll never find any trace of him."

"Well, we have to look for him anyway," I say, fighting off anger and a growing sense of frustration. "What about the police?"

"There are no police, not until you get to Esquintla."

"That's okay, let's call them. Where can I find a telephone?"

"*No hay.*" There isn't one.

"Yes there is," another guard says. "What about Señora Ortíz? Down the mountain?"

"Oh yes, but she charges so much to use it."

"It doesn't matter," I say. "How can I find her?"

Though I have been in Guatemala for six months now, and feel like I know the country well, this town is different. Perhaps it is my role here that is so unusual, but San Francisco de Sales seems surreal and empty in the early night. I almost expect to see tumbleweeds and hear the music from an old Western. We look for food, but no one is working at the tiny store. Someone from our group manages to find us refuge in a family home, and I find everyone there, gathered on the floor, with their wet belongings spread out and hanging off of chairs to dry. A local woman has given Lisa some dry, baggy clothes to wear, and she is huddled on the bed, barely holding it together.

I knock on doors and find a woman to open the store, and she sells us bananas and bread that I take back to the group. Tamara finds the phone at Sra. Ortiz's house. As I walk down the hill to translate, there is hardly any sign of life and a cold wind blows through the streets, swirling trash around in the air. I look up. Overhead the sky is clear, but on Pacaya, the cone is still shrouded in clouds and flickering with silent lightning.

By the time Lisa and Tamara join me at Sra. Ortiz's house with a guidebook and the phone number for the Canadian Embassy, I have done everything I know how to do to find help. I have sent a child running around town to find the police, fire department, and Red Cross phone numbers, and when she comes back we try all three. No one answers. It is like the whole country has gone to sleep and just doesn't care. As I work my way through the touchtone system for the number Lisa is pointing to, I don't have much hope left.

"Canadian Embassy," a woman's voice says in English.

"Hi," I say, relieved. "We need help. We're up on Volcán Pacaya and we've lost a tourist."

"You're on *what?*"

"Volcán Pacaya," I repeat. "The Pacaya Volcano. It was raining and we lost a tourist. He's Canadian. His name is Paul Brace. We need help to find him."

"What country are you in?"

"Uh, Guatemala. What country are *you* in?"

"I'm in Ottawa," she says. My heart sinks. *Really? Canada?* "Tell me again what's happened. Slower this time."

I tell her again, though I know it is a waste of time.

"What were you doing up there in the rain?" she asks.

"I don't think that's really the point," I say. I am getting frustrated now. "The point is that we lost a tourist and we need help."

"How could you *lose* a tourist?"

"You know what…" I take the phone away from my ear and look at the others in the room. "This lady isn't helping."

"Do you want me to talk to them?" Tamara says.

"No, it's alright." I take a deep breath and bring the phone back to my ear. "Look," I say, "are you going to help us or not?"

"Give me a phone number where I can reach you, and I'll make some calls."

Señora Ortíz documents the exact time when I hang up, then asks me for 65 Quetzales (five dollars) for the calls we'd made so far. I reach into my back pocket to pull out my emergency stash. I also find my Fulbright ID badge.

"I forgot I had this," I say, flipping it over. On the back, just below "U.S. Department of State," are the words 24-hour Emergency M.S.O., with a phone number beside it. Immediately I sit down and dial.

"Hello, this is Patrick, what can I do for you?" I am filled with relief at the sound of a familiar name. His voice is soft and sleepy compared to how sterile it was at the embassy in February.

"Patrick, this is Cindy, I don't know if you remember

me. I'm a Fulbright Scholar, and I met you at a security briefing a few months ago."

He says he does. "What can I do for you?"

I take a deep breath. "Ok. Here's the situation. I climbed Pacaya today with a group of tourists from Antigua, and we got caught in a storm at the summit and lost a tourist. We've sent the guards back up a couple of times and tried the police and fire department but no one answers. We're all out of options and we need some help."

I'm nervous he'll scold me like the Canadian woman did. *I told you not to climb Pacaya. Why were you up there in the rain? How could you lose a tourist?* But instead he says, "Okay. Try to take it easy now. I'll get the rescue people out there as soon as possible. I'll bang on doors and wake them up myself if I have to. We'll be there as soon as we can. It'll take us a couple of hours, be we'll be there."

"Thank you. Really?" I say, suspending disbelief for a moment of hope.

"Of course," he says. "Don't worry anymore. We'll take it from here."

Two hours later, people are starting to get restless. It has been too long since we called the embassy and nothing has happened. So, now we are trying another approach, and are bouncing down the road in Antonio's van, heading to the next town so we can bang on the door of the police station and wake someone up.

But just as we leave San Francisco de Sales, we see the convoy with flashing blue and red lights winding up the hill in the distance. As they come closer, we can make out dozens of police and fire vehicles. When they pull up, it seems like there are hundreds of people. The beds of their blue, police pick-up trucks are filled with heavy-duty ropes, fire suits and helmets, and bags of technical climbing gear as though they are ready to climb right down inside the volcano. At the tail end of the procession is Patrick, alone in his black, government Suburban with tinted windows.

I stand next to the open window of the first fire truck and spew out the situation again in Spanish.

"Why don't you get in and tell us on the way," the driver says, opening his door and pulling his seat forward. I squeeze in between the men, with their mustaches and yellow fire suits. The door shuts and the light goes out and we rumble and bounce back up to San Francisco de Sales. I smell their body heat filling up the cabin. I feel the dampness of perspiration condensing on my skin. I see the whites of their eyes as they watch me through the darkness.

At the park entrance, they leap out of the pick-ups and fire trucks and immediately send a wave of rescuers running up the mountain with huge search lights. I answer the questions from Patrick and the Press, who have followed the convoy. Patrick is irritated that I didn't tell him that the tourist was Canadian. "I've already contacted the U.S. State Department. I mean, we would have helped anyway, but…" he trails off.

Once the search is underway, the rest of us don't really know what to do with ourselves, and we wander back into the cement house, where the group is sprawled out on the floor. We wait.

Lisa finally collapses, crying on a cot in the corner and Tamara and Annette rub her back and stroke her hair, and tell her that they're sure we'll find him. I'm starting to be not so sure.

Someone has found some tortillas and a jar of peanut butter, and people are hungrily devouring goopy sandwiches. Some curl up with each other and try to sleep. Some walk outside and look at the stars. Some complain about not being able to go back to Antigua and act like this has all been a huge inconvenience. Some find people to comfort them, and make out under the blankets our host has given us. Some talk, and tell stories and joke about the rats in the rafters.

"Look, there's another one," someone says, giggling

with delight and pointing out a rat.

"In any other situation, they would freak me out, but here they seem almost comforting," someone else adds.

"They're friendly rats," Elena answers, chuckling. "They're like pets."

Someone tells us to keep it down because people in the family who owns the house are trying to sleep.

The minutes crawl by as we wait, and wait, and wait.

At 4:00 in the morning the rescuers finally return and I go out to talk to them. They have found nothing, but they will go back up again in the morning at first light.

As we settle back into the waiting game, I strike up a conversation with a man named Nathaniel. We walk outside and look up at the Milky Way, and I tell him about my Fulbright, and my struggles in Guatemala City, and how I have started to feel really small and pointless in such a big universe, especially since I stopped believing in God.

"But belief in God is the one thing that has lasted for thousands of years," he says. "As an anthropologist, why do you think that is?"

"Maybe it's because nothing else does," I say. "Everything disappears. These houses. These streets. You. Me. Even this volcano. In ten thousand years, none of this will be here. Well, maybe the volcano. But in ten million years, no way." I pause. "So, we need something to cling to and therefore we believe in an afterlife. We have to hope that our spirit somehow lives on, otherwise it is too lonely and meaningless to keep trying. That's why people are so easily tricked into believing that this is all part of some magical being's master plan. But our fear of the end and the unknown can't make it real."

Nathaniel gazes at me with wide, compassionate eyes. "Go on," he says.

"I mean, think about it. Animals don't know they're going to die, and they don't believe in God."

"So, do you think it takes *more* conviction not to believe in God?" he says.

I nod.

"Sounds awfully lonely."

We both look back up at the volcano, at the same time. The lightning has subsided and the clouds are starting to clear.

"I really hope Paul's alright up there," he says, putting his arm around my shoulder. "It sucks to be in such a hostile environment alone."

"Yeah, it does," I say, letting myself lean into his chest and look back at the stars. Above us they are twinkling like they always do, as if nothing in the world is wrong.

RECOVERY

Just before dawn, I finally stop staring helplessly at the volcano and go inside, where I fall asleep for a moment, curled up with my head on Nathaniel's chest. When the second wave of rescuers leave to climb back up the volcano, two of the Americans in our group, Spencer and Douglass, go with them. Tamara agrees to stay behind with Lisa and says she knows enough Spanish to take over with the rescue coordination. I am delirious with fatigue. She thanks me for everything, and tells me to go back to Antigua and rest. I leave my cell number, and ask her to call as soon as she knows anything.

In the van, I sit down next to Elena for the first time since the ordeal began, and she falls asleep instantly, with her head on my shoulder. I lean back against the seat, and pass out with my mouth hanging open. We are all exhausted.

At our hotel, Elena and I shower, and decide we should eat some breakfast. We are walking down the street in Antigua when my cell phone rings.

"They found Paul," Tamara says. "He's coming down now."

"They did? Is he alright?"

"I think so," she says.

"Is he hurt?" I ask.

"I think he's okay," she says.

I can't believe it. I take the phone away from my ear. "He's okay," I burble to Elena, giddy with excitement. "Where was he?" I ask into the phone.

"I don't know all the details," Tamara says, "but I think they found him at the top. They're bringing him down now."

Elena and I are filled with adrenaline, success, and excitement, and we run to breakfast, celebrating. We gorge ourselves on *huevos rancheros,* and are still too excited to sleep, so we walk the streets playing tourist, and I point out all the colonial ruins and take her to the *Convento Santa Clara.* It is one of my favorite places in Antigua because it is so quiet and old, and there is a courtyard with lush flower gardens and hummingbirds buzzing all over the place. We find peace there.

By mid-afternoon, after thinking all day about Paul and Pacaya, and all the things that went wrong last night, we became infuriated at the way the situation was handled by the tour company and Antonio, who was supposed to be in charge of the tour. All night long he had been indifferent to the rescue effort. He had refused to take us in the van to look for help until help was already on the way, and had showed little concern for Paul at all. Elena and I pinpoint a number of big holes in the travel agency's safety net, and decide to go to the office that had run the trip and talk to them about it. Mostly, we want to suggest starting the tours earlier in the day during the rainy season to avoid the rain. Since I have the Spanish to communicate effectively, we think it might be worth a shot.

The woman we speak to obviously has no authority and is just as indifferent to the situation and our chaotic evening as Antonio had been. She says they can't start the tours earlier because people are in Spanish school in the morning.

"They will have to make a choice," I say. "There's no reason people should be on top of a volcano in the rain. It's not safe. If people knew about the danger of lightning, I'm pretty certain they'd be willing to miss a day of Spanish school to go in the morning."

She shrugs. "*No sé*," she says. She doesn't know.

"Safety should be the first concern out there," I say, pleadingly.

She nods in agreement. "Of course."

"It just seems like you shouldn't be running trips in the afternoon in the rainy season," I say.

"Probably not," she says.

Elena and I look at each other and roll our eyes. This is useless.

"Well, at least he's alright," I say, finally.

"Really?" the woman says, looking confused. "I heard that he died."

The air stands still with piercing silence. "No," I say, slowly. "They found him and he was okay."

She lowers her eyes and shakes her head. "No, I don't think so. I think he's dead."

Dead. That word again. It is so final, beginning and ending with such a hard, definitive sound. *Dead. Dead. Dead.*

I repeat it over and over to myself as we run the eight blocks to the hotel where Paul and Lisa are staying, hoping to find someone who can give us some answers. Neither of us want to believe the woman from the travel agency. But my stomach twists with dread and truth. Is it possible? Could he really be... *dead?*

As soon as Elena and I walk into the courtyard, we can feel it in the air. Tamara sees us, puts down her journal, and walks over.

"We heard that Paul is ... dead?" The word squeezes out through my clenched teeth.

She nods. "It's true." She looks at her feet. "It was the

lightning."

"Oh, my god," Elena says softly, her eyes welling up instantly with tears. She turns and drapes her arms around my neck and cries.

I am dry and emotionless after so much up and down. Truthfully, I am unsurprised as I wrap my arms around her and rub her back. I remember him coaching me to the summit, smiling. He wandered off by himself.

"Cindy, that could have been any one of us," she sobs.

"Did he die instantly?" I ask. *Dead. Dead. Dead.* This is Guatemala.

Tamara nods. "Yeah. They think the first bolt of lightning got him, and the second one got the rest of us. Since we were all standing together, we hardly felt it."

I remember the blinding flash and the bang so loud I thought I was dead. I picture myself, crouched with my hands over my ears, terrified. I remember the man crouched under the umbrella. Could the metal frame of that umbrella have attracted the lightning? Or was it the cameras in our bags, or the metal in our wristwatches? Or was it just us, up there, the highest point in a storm? It strikes me that my conversation with Paul was the last one he ever had.

"Lisa said that because of the lightning, 'we all felt the moment he died,'" Tamara says. I imagine him alone in the rain. The crash. The light.

"Where did they find him?" I ask.

"Well, that was why the rescuers had so much trouble. They found his backpack and his shoes off the trail, over around the south side, you know, behind that mound of ash. His shoes were ripped open to the toes."

"And his body?" I say, remembering his big, innocent smile, and the way he waved and blew a kiss down to Lisa before disappearing, even though the clouds blocked the view

"His body was thrown about four hundred meters, over the crater," she says.

I shudder as I realize that this means that his body was flying through the air over our heads, at the moment we were struck.

"They had to climb down the west slope of the volcano to get him, and apparently it was really hard to recover. When they brought him down I saw him." Her voice softens. "He was totally charred. All his clothes had been burnt off."

"Did Lisa see him?"

"No, almost. But it was horrible, because we all thought he was coming down alive."

"That's what you said when you called. What happened?" I say.

"I have no idea. Somewhere along the way the message must have gotten distorted."

I nod. "Typical."

"As soon as I saw them with the stretcher, I knew. Douglass and Spencer were there when they found him and as soon as I saw their faces, I took Lisa away. She's at the Ambassador's house in the capital now, and she's flying home tomorrow morning." Tamara pauses. "But it was really amazing, she was so strong. She said that he was so happy that day. She said he was a true adventurer, and always knew somehow that he would never live to old age. And that if he could have chosen any way to go, this would have been it."

"Struck by lightning on top of an active volcano in Guatemala," I say. "That *is* quite a way to go."

"We should never have been up there in the rain like that," Elena says, wiping her eyes with the back of her hands. "If you ask me, the earth was trying to tell us something."

No one mentions God.

RUNNING AWAY

In the days following Paul's death, Elena and I look for him in the papers and find a bunch of different stories. The *Prensa Libre*, supposedly Guatemala's most reliable newspaper, prints only a three-sentence blurb, and incorrectly says that Paul died from "hypothermia and injuries he sustained." There is no mention of lightning. The *Al Dia* has the most coverage, with a half-page spread and a headline that says "*Se Le Cayó Un Rayo.*" Struck by Lightning. Accompanying the article (which spells his name wrong, calling him Paul Alexander Gomez, instead of Paul Alexander James Brace) is a crude stick-figure diagram, depicting a group of tourists with huge backpacks all getting hit in the head by a dispersed bolt of lightning, and another stick figure getting struck by a single bolt on the other side of the crater, lying down with a pool of blood coming from him.

I think about Lisa all the time. I can't imagine what it would be like to lose someone that you love so much, when until that moment it seems like you both have your whole lives ahead of you. For Elena, it is the realization of vulnerability—that same realization I'd had when Maureen was in the boat accident, that any of us could die at any moment, prepared or not—that has her reeling. For me, it is a sense of utter helplessness I just can't shake, as though we hadn't done enough to save him, even though we know now that he died instantly, and there was nothing we could do to bring him back, short of going back in time and not climbing the volcano at all.

"Let's get out of Guatemala," I say to Elena a few days later. "I can't take it here anymore."

We decide to go to Mexico. But no matter how far we get from Pacaya, part of me stays behind on the volcano, still trying to make sense of things, excavating every moment and thought for deeper meaning. Each time I close my eyes I am there, trapped in that cement house in San Francisco de Sales, waiting, helpless, not able to do anything at all. When we are on buses, traveling long distances, there is a lot of down time, and a lot of time to think too much. During our trip into the Guatemalan highlands, across the border into Chiapas, I stare out the window and stir with anger towards such a system with so many holes that it was impossible to find help without contacting the U.S. embassy, towards the entire falling-apart country of Guatemala, and towards the people themselves for not caring about safety a little more. For shrugging it off like the woman at the travel agency. *Oh really? I heard he died.* Her words echo in my ears.

Slowly, I begin to connect with the weight of Guatemala's deeper grief. After all, when people spend their lives living in fear of the military, watching their family members disappear into the night, hearing gunshots ring out, being forced to work in slave-like conditions, watching their children die from disease and malnourishment, how could they bring themselves to feel compassion for one dead tourist?

During the long, restless nights in youth hostels and cheap hotels, after Elena is asleep, breathing softly beside me, I stare at the shadows on ceilings and see lightning bolts dancing through the darkness, and I begin to accept Paul's death as an act of nature, rather than an act of God.

It is the only thing that makes sense. Death in U.S. culture is hidden from sight. Mangled corpses are zipped into body bags, blood marks on the highway are washed away, sheets are laid over victims of drive-by shootings, and bodies are covered in make-up for funerals and viewings. Many of us live our whole lives, never really knowing what death can do to a person. In a country like Guatemala, on the other hand, death is ever-present. Photos of dead bodies are shown on the front page of every day's newspaper. Everyone has scars. Everyone has stories of accidents, murders, bloodshed. Death is accepted as a part of life. People who die without family connections are left in the street for days until someone is bothered enough by the smell to move them. They are quickly forgotten. The coldness that has made me so terribly lonely and isolated in Guatemala is merely a loss of sensitivity after so much grief. It is easier to accept death if you never let yourself get close to anyone. Indifference to death is a product of desensitization. In a war-torn country, the death of one, or even of 20 is a drop in the bucket. A blink of the eye. It is like an icicle cutting through the heat of this burning land—ever present; a chill in the air, despite the sunshine; a perpetual dryness in the in the back of your throat, despite the humidity; the eerie stillness of a windy day on Lake Atitlán, when the power goes out, dust blows through the streets, and people shut their doors and hide in their houses. So much energy, and so little emotion.

When I try to put all this in perspective with my journey away from faith, Paul's death illuminates the dark, naked reality of the natural world—a place where the earth is a powerful force, and people are creatures just like all the others, part of the food chain, animals who don't want to die. All religion does is make us forget about death, ignore that it happens, lose touch with reality and waste ourselves away working towards a future that may never come. We miss the fleeting precious moments, our one chance, in search of artificial happiness, in the quest for eternal salvation. We overlook the beauty of jade and copper in search of glimmering gold. And in the United States, when people die tragically, for no reason, and we can't make sense of life without them, or why they died so young, all anyone can tell us when we ask *why* is "The Lord works in mysterious ways."

But there is nothing mysterious about the way Paul died. Everything that happened up there made so much sense that it didn't make any sense at all. What *were* we doing up there in the rain? *We were cocky*. We were pushing the limits of the storm without listening to the groans of the earth beneath our feet. *Ignorant. Arrogant*. We pushed too far. *This is the story of man on this planet. When will we learn to listen?*

A lot of people ask me if it was that moment on the volcano that made me not believe in God anymore. It wasn't. But, it did make me feel even more distant, less significant, and like all of us are on the verge of death at any moment. What is the point of anything, if life can end in an instant? Perhaps that is the point of everything.

That moment on Pacaya, when lightning struck so close, the scream that came out of my mouth was from someplace inside of me that I had never been before. For an instant, I truly believed I was *dead*. If you have ever had a moment like this, with a noise so loud, and a flash so bright, and a split second to react or die, you know this place where my scream was born. It was like being punched in the face by a giant fist, pounded by a force so large I couldn't understand at all. It was like being jerked awake by a gunshot going through your chest. In that eternal moment of darkness, when everything stood still and stretched out in front of me, there was a sense of immediate acceptance. *I'm dying. I'm dead*. I didn't have time for the scenes of my life to flash in front of me, or to see that hopeful image of my father waiting in the airport, or to have any regrets. For an everlasting instant, everything was simply over.

I don't think it was God, but there was something huge at work. And it was something larger than I could ever understand.

In the aftermath, the realization that *I* could have died up there strikes both Elena and I quite hard. Part of me is desperate to make amends with God. Maybe all I need to do is put another label on him, like Mother Earth, to find a way to believe again. But I still can't pray because all the history of prayer and forcing religion on people makes me feel like a hypocrite. It is my over-dependence on my faith in times of fear that really turned me away from God in Guate in the first place. I needed to pray because I was weak. The complication of God and religion and prayer only exists because people are weak, and need something to hold onto during the hard times. I see prayer as a sign of ignorance. I see faith as a grand delusion—a trick of the Catholic Church to keep people like me in line.

Lucky for me I am not alone anymore. Elena is here, and even though I can't turn to God anymore, I can turn to her. She can make me strong. Somehow, we can find answers with each other.

"Do you ever feel afraid of death?" I ask her one day, as our bus leaves San Cristobal in Chiapas and head east into the Yucatán Peninsula. "Do you ever get tempted to pray, even though you are an atheist?"

Elena tells me that she has never prayed, and has never felt anything was missing in her life. "I'm not ready to die, but I am also not about to spend my life being afraid that I might. I'd rather live fearlessly and die doing something I love than never do anything at all."

I can't help but think of Paul.

I am utterly grateful for Elena. With her there I don't have as much time to think about how death seem to be chasing me, or to feel afraid. She keeps my mind busy, and her mantra sinks in. She takes my hand and guides me through my twisted maze of fear. She makes me go to parties with people I don't know, makes me meet up with men who ask us out at bars, makes me forget about death on the surface, and truly live for adventure. She ignores the sly gazes of all the crooked-toothed men, she brushes it off when a man walks right up to her on a busy street and sticks his hand in her crotch.

Whatever happens to us, she is fearless. And when I am with her, I am fearless too.

For the next month, Elena and I make an effort not to hold ourselves back. We crave adventure together, and really live. We travel through Belize, back into Guatemala for a short stretch on the eastern coast, and then head on to the Bay Islands in Honduras for two weeks of scuba diving, and flirting with sailors. It is the blissful Central America road trip I always wanted.

By July, I have my Advanced Diver Certification, and have done 19 dives: a shipwreck dive; a cave dive; a night dive with no lights; a deep dive, where I had to do math at 140 feet below surface to experience nitrogen poisoning; a dozen reef-wall dives full of sea turtle, angelfish, and hammerhead sightings; and a navigation dive, during which Elena and I get lost together following an eagle ray, and startle a six-foot barracuda, which charges us from behind a rock. When we surface, we flag down our boat, and tell the German dive instructor, Wolfgang, what happened.

"If you saw a barracuda, you are lucky to be alive," he says, winking. "It could have eaten you like zat!" He snaps his fingers. "You could have died."

"What else is new?" I say, jabbing Elena with my elbow.

Elena just giggles, and says "cool!"

She is completely in her element in Roatán. I have never seen her happier. She glows here. She belongs. I have become so dependent on her company and emotional support that I dread going back to Guatemala, because I know things will be different there. Then one night, fate brings her a Dutch man named Anton, and she falls head over heels, proclaiming that she will stay in Honduras to be with him until her money runs out. She rents a house on the beach, and gets a job at a little café, and promises to meet up with me in San Pedro someday, in a few months, before heading home. We say goodbye, and I head back to Guatemala, alone again.

Along the way, I stop at the Mayan ruins of Copán in northern Honduras. There are few people at the archaeological site, and after my month of bouncing all over the place and trying to keep up with Elena, the ruins have the still peace of a cemetery. Monkeys chatter as they swing on vines, a chorus of bird song fills the trees, and the carved stones, temples, and stelae peer out from beneath a layer of soft, wet moss. At first they are hidden, but when I squint my eyes I see faces and figures carved in stones emerging from the jungle. Copán is known as one of the most artistic of the Mayan sites, and a wealth of anthropological knowledge has come from the artwork and hieroglyphs at this site. However, to me the most intriguing element of this particular Mayan city is its network of underground tunnels. When I am there, the tunnels are closed to the public, but I peer into one, as far as I can see, and it is black, damp, dark.

I imagine the Mayans of 500 years ago, with torches and baskets of food, jade, and cloth, squinting in the darkness, wondering if Pedro de Alvarado will find them. I imagine them navigating underground, using their network of passageways to escape the conquistadors, and the landowners who came later looking for slaves to work on their plantations. Did they know what was coming? Did they get away?

There are rumors of tunnels in the hills around Lake Atitlán where the Tz'utujiil Maya hid during the conquest, and also where they hid from Rios Montt and his "scorched earth" campaign in the 1980s. During this bloody time, the Maya of Lake Atitlán were somewhat spared because of their remote location. But towards the end of the violence, the military found them anyway.

Between 1982 and 1983, during the 17 months that Rios Montt led as dictator, the military carried out a campaign against bands of leftist guerillas in the Mayan Highlands. Entire villages were wiped out with extreme brutality. They killed all the women and children along with the men. Homes were burned. 600 villages were wiped off the map and, overall, 200,000 people were killed or disappeared. *Ancianos* in San Pedro have told me of hiding in the tunnels around Atitlán, of stocking caves with supplies, and hunkering in the dark, praying that the military did not find them. They have told me about large tunnels that run across the country, from one side to the other, which they will use for escape, if they ever have to. These tunnels are considered sacred ground.

For some reason, I think of Paul, and how that lightning struck so hard, leaving his shoes, ripped open to the toes. Leaving scorched earth behind as his body flew over the volcano. I think about the woman at the travel agency. *Oh really? I heard he died.* I think about Maureen's boat accident and how the boat captain lied and told me no one died, about leaving that woman without her arm, bleeding on the lakeshore. I think of how much one death has affected me. Then I think of what it means to hide in the darkness, scared for your life, without knowing the reason. I think of a family, awakened in the middle of the night by the sound of heavy boots, and the metallic clicking of guns. Watching a husband, or a brother, or a son, yanked from his bed, taken away, and never seen again. I think about the mass graves, the one near Rabinal, and the lakeshore at Atitlán. I think of 200,000 people, dead in one year, because of one man. I try to imagine how many people that is, and I can't. But suddenly, I understand that they cannot feel sympathy for *one* death or *one* injury. Not when they have lost so many. Their load of grief is already too heavy, and they have turned to stone. They cannot carry any more.

SMOKING JESUS

Back in San Pedro, my things are right where I left them, and I slip into my old routine. I try to tell myself that it is nice to be alone after being around so many people for so long, and I find quiet on the rocks, in my herbal teas, in my books, and in my yoga. Time moves slowly, and I have nowhere to be. I try to get used to it again, and I look for magic in sunrises and sunsets, and moonrises, and I spend enough nights gazing at the Milky Way that I know how to tell time by the position of the stars in the sky.

But within a week, being alone quickly turns into lonely. Time turns into too much time, and even though I have anthropology to do, and D'Noz, and Kayla, I find myself without a real purpose. I don't know what I am looking for, but I know that I'm looking for something. Meaning.

During the rainy season, rains come in every afternoon, turning pathways into streams, and roads into rivers. Cases of amoebas and giardia flare up all over San Pedro because of the pollution in the lake water. Everything flows downhill and empties into Atitlán, taking with it silt, human and animal waste, and trash. Especially during the rainy season, each drop of water in the lake is loaded with a plethora of microorganisms, just longing to find warm, moist host environments in which to reproduce by the thousands.

All of the water that is used for showers, toilets, faucets, and irrigation comes directly from the lake without being treated. No one claims it is potable, but they do use it to wash dishes and sometimes vegetables at a restaurant. This means that even the tiniest drop of water left on a glass or lettuce leaf, or a careless ice cube could spell disaster. Most travelers who have read their guide book know not to eat raw vegetables or ask for ice at a restaurant, and stick only to things like bananas that can be peeled, leaving coleslaw and cucumber garnishes untouched on their plates. But some eat indiscriminately and pay the price. Travelers are often intelligent enough to drink bottled water, but sometimes they forget not to let any shower water dribble into their mouths. And often, they swim right next to the shore, where the pollution is at its worst.

Sooner or later, everyone gets sick.

Sometimes the bug hits right after eating something suspicious, but sometimes the amoebas sneak in undetected and stay quiet for two weeks before thousands of eggs hatch in your intestines.

Until realizing what is going on, I am confused, because I have been low and under-the-weather for days, despite the meditation and health food and tea. Despite my yoga, I've been cranky and I get irritated with the incessant pounding of hammers, and shouting in Tz'utujiil. I hate Guatemala and can't wait to go home, and I think it is me. I tell myself to suck it up and deal with it, because this is a once-in-a-lifetime opportunity, and I might not get a chance to enjoy life this way ever again. But as hard as I try to stay positive, everything annoys me beyond belief, and I *can't wait to get out of this god-forsaken shit-hole.*

Even though I always pinch my mouth shut religiously in the shower, I get sick.

Even though I am always careful to use only purified water to wash my vegetables, and to dry my dishes thoroughly, because I know that even a drop of lake water left on a glass could lead to intestinal demise, I get sick.

Even though I am trying to know San Pedro from the inside, and trying to feel like I belong here, I get sick.

Two weeks after I return to San Pedro, I am cramped up and doubled over, cursing Guatemala through my teeth.

The discovery of epazote is what saves me. This remedy is an herb and a relative of wormseed, and is tremendously effective compared to Cipro and other antibiotics. Epazote is administered as an infusion, and is made by boiling a handful of leafy stalks in water for 15 minutes, then drinking the resulting pungent tea. While it does not taste very good, it is so effective that you can literally hear it working within seconds of swallowing. Your stomach starts gurgling and churning almost instantly, and your mood miraculously improves. You drink this tea three times in one day to eliminate the first round of amoebas, and repeat again in two weeks to eliminate their eggs. It is cheap, gentle, and a secret that is only given out to those who have been accepted here.

When I go to Solar Pools to stock up on epazote from their garden, I meet Amber. "I could use a dose too," she says, and invites me to sit with her and drink our tea together in the garden.

Amber is Australian, bubbly, rosy-cheeked, and full of humor. We talk for hours, the way travelers can, about my trip, my experience on Pacaya, and my voyage through Mexico, Belize, and Honduras with Elena. And she tells me about her motorcycle journey through the Western Hemisphere, the book she is writing called "A Chick's Guide to the Americas," and some flirty boys she met along the way. Soon, I am telling her about what it is like to come back to San Pedro, and the Fulbright project I have ahead of me. I mention my big atheism decision, the

114

search for answers, and how the hardest part now is the loneliness, and how no matter how many people I am near, I can't seem to shake it.

"I just want to go home," I say. "And I wish I didn't because I've wanted to come live in Central America my whole life. I know I'd regret it if I did leave, and I have a project to finish. But it doesn't change the sense of longing I feel for stupid American things, like my car, or a toasted bagel with cream cheese."

"What you need, Chickadee, is some roomies," Amber says, once I've gotten everything out. "So why don't you move in with us?"

When I arrive at the house with my bags, Amber is on the couch, rolling a joint. She points me to my bedroom, and motions towards the bathroom with her head. "Watch out for the toilet seat in there. It's not connected. Also, the spider's name is George."

"And what about this guy?" I say, pointing to a plastic mold of Jesus. Someone has taken it off the wall and put it on the table.

"He freaked me out, so I took him down," says the third housemate, a blonde woman with lipstick and pigtails. She emerges from the bathroom and straightens her skirt. "I mean, we sure as hell aren't going to worship it."

Amber says Cathy is from Canada "recovering from marriage."

"Did you tell her about the dogs?" Cathy says.

"That's the Dude," Amber says, pointing to a gray mutt in the corner, nursing seven puppies. "We're trying to potty train them, so as soon as they're done eating, we'll have to watch. Just pick 'em up and chuck 'em outside if they start to piss."

I take my bags into my room where I throw them down on the foam mattress. The window over the bed looks out onto the Elementary school playground and the giant mural of a volcano with a dove above it, and the words "Jesus is the Lord of San Pedro".

When I come back into the living room, Amber and Cathy are chasing the puppies around, waiting for each one to start peeing, so they can chuck it outside. This is easy to do because the living room has wide doors that open to the garden. Cathy catches one just as he starts, and scoops him up, mid-pee. She plops him outside the door, where he finishes his business, and she coos "good buuoooooooy!"

Amber lights up the joint, then picks up the Jesus with her other hand. "I have so many sinful thoughts!" She giggles. "Here, Jesus, have a toke."

"We could drill a hole in his mouth and turn him into our own private Maximón shrine," I say.

"That's a bloody great idea," Amber says. "Cath, grab a knife from the kitchen."

I sit down next to Amber on the couch and she offers me the joint. I hesitate, but reach for it anyway.

"Sorry mate, do you smoke?" she says. "I should have asked."

"I have smoked before, in the past, but never here. I'm paranoid about ending up in Guatemalan prison. What about the *policía*?"

"Please, chickadee," Amber says. "The cops here smoke more dope than we do. Besides, if they give you any trouble, just give them some Quetzales." She offers it to me again, and we smoke, gazing out at the chickens pecking their way up our long yard.

Cathy brings the knife from the kitchen and the wind begins to blow suddenly. The garden door swings open with a bang. Overhead, thunder rumbles. Beyond the cornfield, there are whitecaps on Lake Atitlán and the water is a dark, ominous, churning gray. "At least they're not pooping yet," Cathy says, throwing a rag onto a new puddle on the floor and squeezing onto the couch.

Amber uses the knife to perform surgery on plastic

Jesus. Cathy gets out a cigarette so that we can make the mouth hole the right size. Within a few minutes, it is up on the wall, and I am bleary-eyed and giggling with stony delight.

"We're not going to offend anyone with this, are we?" I say, referring to Jesus.

"No worries, chickadee," Amber says. "We'll hang a bandana over it when the locals come by. Everyone else will love it. We can pull it off for shock value when we have parties." When she finishes, she slides the cigarette into the hole and holds the head at arm's length to admire her work. Then she climbs up onto the sofa and hangs it up so it looks down over the living room and through the doors into the yard.

"It's awesome," I say. "I think I am finally relaxing. This is just what I needed."

"Jesus, you look like *you* need to relax," Cathy says, taking her cigarette back. "Here, take a hit of this." She takes the joint from Amber's mouth, re-lights it, and sticks it into the mouth hole. "There. That should chill him out." She takes it back, sucks on it and passes it to me. "That is fucking symbolic," she coughs.

"Brilliant, mate," Amber says, as I pass her the joint. She puts an unlit cigarette in Jesus' mouth and gazes at him with glistening eyes. "Absolutely fucking brilliant. That is a work of art and belongs in a museum."

That afternoon, it pours, and I write poems about cleansing rain in my journal. I do yoga poses and burn sage in my new bedroom to cleanse the energy, and the weed leaves me tired and loopy, so I lie down to take a nap. When I wake up, it is dark outside, and riotous laughter is coming from the living room. I open the door and see a dozen people milling around and drinking vodka and orange juice. Amber is on the sofa snorting a line of cocaine off a piece of broken mirror, and Cathy is next to her with a dog in her arms, painting its toenails red.

"Hey! Cindy's up!" Amber shouts. "Hey everyone, this is our new American roomie!"

Everyone cheers and raises their plastic cups in the air. Someone pours me a drink, and before I know it I am seated between Amber and Cathy, holding the dog still so Cathy can get her back toenails. Each time someone new arrives, Amber rips the bandana off the Smoking Jesus for them, and the crowd collapses in laughter over their shock. Soon, there is a line of glistening white powder laid out in front of me, and Amber is giving me instructions. "Pinch one side of your nose shut and do half. Then do the other half in the other nostril. Evens it out that way. Just sniff in real hard and fast."

The cocaine era at the house is the beginning of a whole new way of life, not because the drug makes me particularly high, or because it feels particularly good, but because there are friends and a community and a party life that go with it. There is a freedom, a sense of rebellion that I have never let myself have before. The high itself is a bit of a letdown, like sex was the first time after all the hype. But the fact that I am "doing cocaine" is thrilling beyond belief.

In the beginning, all I can think is that I am not the kind of girl anyone would expect this kind of behavior from. I was second chair flute in the college orchestra, desperate to please my teachers and my parents. I sang in the gospel choir and said my prayers at night before I went to bed. I studied for my tests, and I got A's on my papers, and here I was in Guatemala as a Fulbright scholar. No one I knew at home would accept the fact that I had "done cocaine." I would surely be ostracized, and there would eventually be some sort of intervention for what people would undoubtedly assume was a "drug problem."

But opening the door to drugs is like releasing a secret part of myself. It is like unleashing that side of me that snuck out of my house at night in high school to be with my boyfriend in his parents' basement—the wild child no one knows about. I see suddenly, how much I have held myself back all these years, trying to be a good Christian girl, and how much I long to break free from all of society's rules about what is right and what is wrong. I'm tired of staying between the lines.

"You're too hard on yourself, Chickadee," Amber says. "Now that your finally free from the bleedin' Church, it's bout time to have a smidge of fun."

Cocaine flows through Casa Shag like it is cartel headquarters. One day, an English guy named Angus shows up with LSD, MDMA, and something he calls 2CB. "I don't really know what it is," he says. "Some guy drew me a picture on a napkin with molecules and electrons and everything. I think it's like acid with mescaline. Whatever it is, Love, it'll open you up to a brilliant new way of thinking." He sweeps his hand theatrically across the sky as he says it, looking like someone who might have once been in a band. "There's also opium, crystal meth, and heroine, and all you gotta do is ask the right people." He winks and jabs me in the ribs. "If you wanted to make ten thousand dollars you could even swallow a bunch of cocaine and take it back to the States. I know a guy who could set it all up. I'll introduce you if you want."

I don't take Angus up on his offer, but Cathy signs up to make a run across Mexico with 5 kilos of brick weed in her backpack for $500.

In San Pedro, marijuana is available by the trash-bag-full. There is so much of it and it is so cheap that people who are headed for the border leave pounds of it behind. After rolling a joint, instead of picking up every precious leaf that falls out like they would in the States, where it costs so much that each speck of green is like a golden nugget, they simply blow the leftovers off the table and onto the floor. July in San Pedro means that pot is *always* in the air, lingering thick and sweet in the corners of every room, everywhere.

I ease into it slowly. Because I grew up in the age of D.A.R.E., and school drug awareness programs that terrified the crap out of kids at the tender ages of eight or nine, I am still a little scared of cocaine and acid and anything else because of how addictive I think "hard drugs" are—like if I do anything in that category more than once, I'll automatically become a crack-head and San Pedro will swallow me forever. I am partially afraid I might wake up one day to find out I have an addictive personality after all, and I am just like Dave, and Primo, and Charlie, wandering around San Pedro with no shoes and nothing to do with my life other than get high.

But I read *Fear and Loathing in Las Vegas*, and fall in love with Hunter S. Thompson. Then, I see the movie and fall in love with Johnny Depp. I read *The Teachings of Don Juan* by Carlos Castaneda, and I become fascinated with the idea of peyote, hallucinogenic flying trips, and anything that will give me a new experience.

"The human brain is capable of so many things, and we use so little of it," Angus says one day, while we are sharing a joint in the living room. "Just imagine what you could do if you tap in to a higher level of consciousness!"

So, I open myself to everything, and indulge in the name of experimentation, anthropology, and wanting to see the world in a new light. And in the beginning, while everything is still glowing, I am careful not to overdo it.

But there are so many drugs and so many parties, and they just keep coming my way. Soon, I am smoking pot a lot. Nothing really gives me any reason to be scared, because I have days when I don't smoke, and I'm fine, so I know I don't *need* it. But with all this loneliness and searching, and not knowing who I am, it helps me forget about all my questions and fears. When I'm stoned, I have friends who make me laugh. I smoke and write poems and songs, and make inspired anthropological observations, and I sit on the rocks and watch the waves, and Lake Atitlán feels welcoming, like a home.

On these lazy, hazy afternoons—when the breeze is just right, and the reeds sing, and the waves lap against the shore, when the fishermen stand silhouetted in their *cayukos*, casting nets out into the water, and the women wash their *cortes* and *huipiles* on the rocks, and the air is filled with wood smoke and children's laughter and the tapping of pestles—I am totally at peace. I want to stay in San Pedro smoking weed forever.

SEX, DRUGS, AND BITCHES IN HEAT

"Where's Charlie?" I ask Dean one morning, as I sit down on the balcony of his restaurant with my coffee. Dave is there, and Primo is downstairs with Crazy Mario, but Charlie is not in his usual spot at the bar, already slurping tequila.

"Didn't you hear?" Dean says. "Charlie died."

"He *died?*" I swallow.

"Yup. Had a seizure one day in the bathroom and whacked his head on the loo. He was epileptic, you know."

"That and a lot of other things," Dave grunts. He nods at Dean. "*Litro?*" he says, bowing slightly and sitting with a nod, his Moses beard swishing across the bar.

Dean pops the cap off a liter bottle of Gallo beer, pours a shot of Jack Daniels, and rolls his eyes at Dave. "I still don't know how you can start drinking this early. We just opened."

"Start?" Dave says, snorting. "Why would you ever stop?"

"How long ago did this happen?" I say.

"What? Charlie? This weekend," Dave says. "Primo found 'im. All bloodied up an stiff as a rock. Hadta go to the bank in Pana to find out his last name so's we could call his folks. They didn't care much. Wouldn't send money to have his body shipped home. It's buried up the hill. Kind of a fiasco if you ask me." He tilts the whiskey back and drains it with a swallow. As he sets it down on the bar, his eyes are glassy, and the animation vanishes from his face. He doesn't say anymore, just stands up with his liter of beer and walks outside.

Later, when I see Dave again, on the veranda of Sid's place on the less-touristy, expat side of town, he is accusing Primo of giving him a foot fungus which is slowly eating his insides alive. "I'll be dead in a year," he says. "All cuz I lent that black bastard my shoes."

"Watcher mouth," Sid shouts from the garden, where he is clawing randomly at the ground with a Mayan-style hoe. "That's racist. This is a *Christian* house." Sid is a beer-bellied, bald Vietnam Vet from Texas, who has been in San Pedro for years, starting up business after business, and failing miserably each time. His current project is growing organic lettuce, and it seems to be the first line of work that is turning a profit for him. He provides lettuce to a few gringo-run restaurants and feels like he's making ends meet and life is good, "just as long as I got whiskey in the cupboard and smokes in my pocket."

I like Sid's veranda. I like to sit there scribbling their dialogue in my notebooks, because everyone knows I am writing about San Pedro. They want to be in my book, so they talk a lot about all the drugs they do, and how they don't care for America any more. The people of San Pedro don't judge, they say, so they're here to stay. Right on the edge of the footpath that runs through this corridor of restaurants and hostels, the veranda is a crossroads, and a great place to conduct interviews with expats, get information on the local drug trade, surround myself with characters who make me laugh, and people-watch. I stop in each time I pass by, and usually justify my daily visits there as part of my Fulbright research. I watch everything that happens with an observer's eye, and attempt to dig into the heart of what makes San Pedro such a moody, strange, and contradictory place. I write down exactly what people say.

"Anybody got a joint?" Dave says. He pulls out a chair and plants himself at the table, where he pours together leftover rum and coke from last night to make a Cuba Libre.

I shake my head and nod towards Sid with my chin.

"–ere," Sid says, handing him a smoldering roach, pinched between two fingers.

"Cool," Dave says, sucking it down. "I'll roll a new one." He puts it out, fishes a bag out of his pocket, and starts rolling a fresh joint. Along the path, the police stroll by, hands resting on their batons.

"Shit, put that away," Angus says, pointing to the cops.

"Eh, don't worry about it," Sid says. He stands up and waves to them. "*Buenos días amigos*" he shouts. They look up at him with indifference and keep walking. Sid sits back down laughing, then makes himself a drink. "They can't do shit," he says. "Ain't nothin' in the world compared to the freedom you get here, boy." He stands, pulls his shirt off and rubs the gray hair on his belly, then walks over to a marijuana plant growing just inside the fence and brushes his fingers across the leaves.

"You really can do whatever you want around here, can't you?" I say, scribbling in my notebook.

"That's right we can!" Sid says, shouting suddenly. "We're mother-fucking lettuce growers!" He slams his drink down on the table and stomps into the garden, where he picks up the hoe and starts clawing.

"Hey," Dave says loudly, pacing back and forth in the yard. It is just past noon, and as usual he is already high and drunk. "Did you hear they're pulling more bodies out of Lake Amatitlán, down in Esquintla?"

"Really?" Angus says half-heartedly, as though by now everyone there knows that bodies in Guatemala aren't really news.

"Yup. They've got three already. But there's probably a bunch more. Sounds like the police have somebody and they're giving up gang secrets."

"How deep is that lake?" I ask.

"Deep enough to hold bodies," Dave says, sneering at me.

"Yeah, but not as deep as this one," Angus says, leaning back against the wall.

"You know the only way to ever recover bodies from one of these lakes is when they float up," Sid shouts from the garden.

"God, with all the violence here, there's probably 100,000 bodies in this lake," I say. "Sometimes I feel like it's haunted." I catch Angus' eye and he winks at me.

"Probably is," he says. "Did I tell you what happened to me the other day?"

I shake my head.

"Well, I was with the Shaman's daughter, Jocela, and she said she was sensing a lot of jealousy around me."

"Uh-huh."

"Well, you know Helen, the hustler? She thinks that she's my girlfriend, and she has been really jealous whenever I even look at anyone else. I told Jocela about Helen and she lit a black candle and started chanting, and said it would protect me. Then, when I got back here at one in the morning, Helen was here in my bed, and I told her about it, and she freaked out and jumped up and started sprinkling water on the floor outside the door."

"That's weird," I say, scribbling. Later, I look up candles in the Mayan tradition and learn that black is the color for enemies and vengeance.

"Yeah, but get this," he says, talking too fast. "The next day Jocela came up to me and said she wasn't feeling well. She said 'Last night the strangest thing happened to me. For no reason at all I woke up at one in the morning vomiting water.'"

"Whoa," Dave says. "Helen's a witch, man. I

wouldn't touch that girl even if my dick was twelve feet long."

"That is crazy," I say.

"Yeah, it is," Sid adds, still yelling from the garden. "Besides, you've gotta slit the belly first if you want 'em to sink right."

"What?" I say.

"The bodies. Otherwise after a few days, they'll float to the top."

There is a moment of silence. "How do you know that?" I say.

He looks up from his hoe and shrugs. "My training."

Some days, I spend long hours just sitting, contemplating things. I call my mother and tell her I am "on a journey of self-discovery," though I don't tell her about the fact that I've tried cocaine and will probably do some acid soon. I write pages and pages in my journal every day, and wander through town taking notes, and striking up conversations with the locals about the past, the future, and the lingering grief from the war that doesn't really seem to be over.

Amber and Cathy quickly find boyfriends, and every night when I come home things are quiet except for the quiet moaning sounds coming from behind their closed doors. They nickname our house "Casa Shag." I start working more nights behind the bar at D'Noz, partially for something to do, mostly to meet everyone coming through town and to observe the expat-local dynamic for my project. Even living with the girls, I am lonely. I don't know why I can't enjoy myself more, but every night in my journal I write about wanting to go home, even though this is supposed to be the dream come true. I start to hear noises at night. Packs of wild dogs howling. The sound of someone walking across the roof. Chickens rustling through the buses in the yard. The sound of screaming. Candles flicker in rooms with no breeze. The wind picks up and drives at us so hard that the locals have a name for it. *It is the Xocomil,* they say, *the fabled wind. Time to stay inside.* The electricity cuts off and the lights stay out for days. By the end of August, I am convinced that there is energy at work here. The lake is alive and has the moods of a bitter woman scorned.

I watch Amber and Cathy work through the men in town, letting them go just as quickly as they arrive, and I want a man in my life. But most of the guys who pass through are just looking for drugs and sex. They come and sit down next to me at bars and at the veranda every night, and they spout poetry, and touch my skin, and try to kiss me, and say cheesy things like, "I can see inside you. You are like seagull, always looking for beaches and never finding them." But no one in Guatemala can see inside of me, and all these men want is a one-night stand. No one I meet has any idea who I really am, or has any real interest in getting to know me. Sometimes, when I do find someone who isn't leaving in the morning and is easy to talk to, I tell that person everything about me. But they still don't get it when I get to the part where I admit that I want to go home.

"Why would you want to go *there*?" they scoff, making me feel ashamed and overly-American.

They can't understand how someone who smiles and laughs as much as I do, has grant money and food in her stomach, and lives in a place like San Pedro, can be lonely or depressed. They don't understand how someone with a full life can feel so empty. Neither do I.

The music pounds in my temples and everyone gets up to dance with me. Candles flicker on the tables, incense burns and the wind howls in through the windows. Joints are floating through the crowd, I feel the music pulsing in my blood, and move like no one is watching—like I am an Indian belly dancer with a perfect brown body and silky black hair. I feel people moving around me, but the world outside disappears. Amber and Cathy and I slip into the D'Noz bathroom and each do another line off the back of the toilet. My nose goes numb, and I rub my finger on my gums, tasting the bitterness of the cocaine on the back of my throat.

I want to get higher. I want more. When I am like this, sweating and moving and forgetting, everything seems so real. I forget about amoebas, and fear, and getting shocked by electric showers, and clothes that never dry, and having to throw used toilet paper in a trash can covered with flies because the pipes can't handle it. I just dance, and I feel my body move to the pounding rhythm of the drums. And I love it here.

"You need to get laid," Cathy says into my ear.

"Yes. You do," Amber says. "Desperately."

Instead, we three girls dance together until the music stops.

There is a man at the bar with sweet brown eyes and curly hair, sitting alone. I am working the morning shift, and no one else is in the restaurant yet. He orders coffee.

I make enough for both of us, and sit on a stool, facing him. He is cute. Clean-shaven. Deep green eyes that look sensitive, and intelligent. He asks about me, and says his name is Christopher.

I tell about Pacaya. I tell about my Fulbright, about Guatemala City, and he listens. He nods like he actually knows what a Fulbright is, and I am relieved to have an intelligent, non-drunken conversation with someone smart. "What about you?" I say.

He is a doctor. He has just arrived from Boston for a year of work at the clinic up in town, and when I put the mug of coffee down in front of him, he lets his hand graze across mine. "I like your freckles," he says. "They're beautiful."

Inside, I dance and leap twelve feet in the air.

He doesn't let go of my hand until Dave comes in

and sits down beside him. I serve his shot of whiskey and liter of beer and Christopher and I talk about anthropology, the Mayan people, religion, and faith. I open myself up to him. "I don't know why I feel so homesick," I say. "Here I am in paradise, and all I want to do is go home."

"It makes perfect sense," he says, smiling sweetly. "You lost your faith in God. You carved a huge hole in your safety net. Of course you feel lonely. Of course you feel scared. You just have to find a way to fill the gap. Shouldn't be too hard around here. This place is fascinating."

"I should just focus on my Fulbright project," I say.

"That's a great idea," he says, finishing off the last sip of his coffee and standing up. "Put your energy into something productive. It's amazing how much better you'll feel."

"You leaving?" I say, clearing his mug and wiping down the counter.

"Gotta go to work," he says, looking at his watch. "Clinic opens soon. I hate to go, but I'm sure I'll see you again."

"I hope so," I say.

He smiles. "Me too," he says.

I watch him walk away with a dull ache throbbing in my chest. *That's him.* I say to myself. *That's the one I want. Christopher*

Every morning now, I wake up at dawn to the out-of-tune honking of a three-dozen piece brass band, a quivering marimba, and snares and cymbals and bass drums that rattle the windows with an uneven pulse—the children's Evangelical School marching band practicing diligently for the upcoming Independence Day celebration on September 15. I try to sleep in with my earplugs, but flies dive bomb my face, mosquitoes bite my arms, and the dogs yap so persistently that Amber shouts sailor curses at them from her bedroom. It is impossible to have a quiet morning here, and we are staying up so late that none of us are getting enough sleep. We are starting to snap at each other, acting crazy, like bitches in heat.

All the coke has made my nose raw, and I am tired of drinking, so I have decided to take a break from everything. Meeting *Christopher* inspired me to get my act together with my Fulbright, if only to pass the time more productively, so I am avoiding Amber and Cathy and the party scene, going to be earlier at night, getting up and doing yoga, eating healthy, and actually doing my fieldwork. I read books on Guatemalan history, I sit in town and take notes on things I see happening. Five mornings a week I volunteer at the Museo Tz'utujiil, helping a man named Augustín catalogue his library in exchange for Tz'utujiil language lessons, and his services as translator, during interviews he arranges for me with Mayan *ancianos*.

Suddenly, I have a busy schedule. Tuesday and Thursday afternoons I take Kayla to Solar Pools for a hot bath and to D'Noz for dinner. Monday, Wednesday, and Friday nights, I work the bar at D'Noz. And Saturday mornings, I interview a woman named Ada at her house up outside of town on the slope of the volcano. We walk to the market together, buy vegetables, and she teaches me how to really bargain, and soon I am getting the local prices, and I am interviewing the women who work the market-stalls.

Ada buys all her produce from a child-sized, *anciana* named Cecilia. Cecilia is a gem. She is tiny and sweet, and each time she sees me, she acts as though I am the long-lost granddaughter she has never met. "*Ay! Chula!*" she squeals, when she sees me. She climbs up on a stool and leans across her market table to embrace me, and holds me tight, touching my face with her soft wrinkled hands, and kissing me lightly on the cheek. "*Tan gusto ver*te, *m'ija*," she says. So good to *see* you, my child. "*Como estaaás?*" I love the way these women accent their Spanish, drawing out the syllables, singing them so melodically, with so much emphasis in the strangest places. She gives me good prices, and each time she drops it down a quetzal, she says, *"por ser tan buen amiga."* For being such a good friend. She sends me off with a gentle, *"que Diós te cuida, mi niña."* May God watch over you, my girl.

I am touched by her kindness, and sad for her spirit. I feel this way every time someone talks about God this way—almost sorry for them, sorry that they live with such strong belief in something that I know isn't real. Won't death be such a letdown to them, when there is no heaven? And I still don't understand how it is these people believe such a combination of things. They are Christian by appearance, wearing crosses, attending mass, and pledging allegiance to Jesus. But they are almost pagan in practice, worshiping complex idols like Maximón, telling me in interviews about the spirits of the lake and of the animals, the personality of the wind, the wrath of the earth and all its gods, *characoteles*, sorcerers, and *brujas*.

Tz'utujiil oral tradition is laden with these characters. There is a father-sun, mother-moon ideology, and an almost Oriental quality to the ideas of balance, harmony, and connectedness with each other and with the earth. Like yin and yang. But, like Angus' experience with the black candles and the Shaman's daughter, there is a sense of dark magic. There is less emphasis on health, mindfulness, and well-being than there is in Eastern religion, and instead there is almost a psychedelic twist to the stories people tell me. Perhaps it is all the drugs flowing through town. Perhaps the entire population has a contact high, and all these ghosts and witches they speak of are just figments of massive hallucinations. Or perhaps the witchcraft, and dark magic of this town makes it a better place to get high, a place where a psychedelic vision could be the answer I've been seeking, where drugs are like opening the doorways to spirituality all over again.

In the evenings, when I don't have to work, I go to Sid's veranda where I tell everyone the stories I've heard, and eventually get drunk. Then I switch from writing, to singing at the top of my lungs with Neilz or Heishbert, two Danish hippies who often come by with guitars. One night I sing Bobby McGee, just like Janis Joplin, and everyone realizes I have a voice. They start giving requests, and soon men I don't even know are sitting closer, and touching my legs. Angus comes home from work at Café Muchies, and greets me with a kiss on the cheek. "I brought you something," he says. "Open your mouth."

The tab tastes like cardboard on my tongue. Before the acid kicks in, we all wander across the path to a bar called Barrio, where we order hamburgers and Cubas, and sit around the campfire in the yard. A pack of dogs charges by along the path, chasing a terrified female mutt, and I look up to see the full moon glaring down over the volcano. It throbs in the sky, pulsing with the blood in my temples, lunging at me, staring like an angry parent.

The dogs always go crazy during the full moon. They appear in the shadows like demons, and challenge us with their stares. They charge anyone who shows fear, attacking tourists. For the past week, a truck has been driving around town announcing a poisoning, warning people to keep their dogs close because on the night of the full moon, they will throw poisoned meet into all the fields. Supposedly they will not poison dogs that have an orange collar, saying that they have gotten a rabies shot, but no one really trusts that promise. All the dogs that are out right now are strays, and they are crazy and aggressive. I have taken to carrying rocks in my pocket, or a chunk of firewood clenched in my fist. It makes me feel better just to have a weapon in my hand.

"If they attack, you have to make yourself big," a woman says, sitting next to me at the campfire. She is wearing traditional Mayan dress, but her voice has no hint of an accent. "You have to find the leader of the pack and scare the piss out of him." My head starts to feel light, and I hold my hands right up to the fire, spreading my fingers, watching the flame lick my skin. "My god girl, take care of your skin!" the woman shouts suddenly. "Don't let it bake like a goddamn pork chop!"

When I jump, she laughs so hard at me that her face goes bright red. Then she pulls out a huge joint and says her name is Cheryl.

She lights it and passes it to me, then gets up and wanders off, leaving me with the entire thing burning between my fingers. I stare into the fire and watch it dance in time with the music. I think the acid is starting to kick in.

"Can I have some of that?" someone says, his voice deep, sexy, and familiar. Christopher, the doctor, sits down beside me.

"Of course," I say.

And then, before I know what is happening, Christopher makes me laugh. Then his hand is on my thigh, then it is brushing across my face as his lips meet mine. I keep my eyes open and the acid melts his features together, so it seems like I am kissing a lump of melted marshmallows. My mouth goes dry, and I have no saliva to share with him. He gives me a sip of his beer. "Let's get out of here," he says, taking my hand and helping me stand. I twirl down the footpath beside him, dancing to music that isn't there, though he says he can hear it, just by watching me. I wish I hadn't taken that acid. I am acting like a fool.

I take him to Casa Shag and bring blankets out into the garden. We sit, leaning against each other, and he massages my back and shoulders, while I stare at the moon. We talk for hours, keeping each other warm with our body heat, and as the acid peaks, my mouth starts to feel wetter and sweeter against his. Then, at the moment when the moon is highest in the sky, he pulls off my shirt and starts kissing my collar bone. He is so gentle to me, wrapping his whole soul around my body in the moonlight. When it is over, just before dawn, with the roosters already crowing, we fall asleep together, my head resting on his shoulder, his arm softly stroking my back, our breathing in perfect unison with the lapping of the waves on the rocks.

CULTURAL DIFFERENCES

San Pedro celebrates independence on September 15th, along with the rest of Guatemala, but for the people here, it is more than a chance to celebrate freedom from Spanish oppression. It is a chance to remember history and tell stories from the past, to celebrate their heritage and their Mayan ways, and to make a plea to the younger generation to conserve customs. In the days leading up to the festival, my interviews are filled with tales of ancestors, spirits, tragedies, and wistful accounts of how things used to be.

I sit in sparsely-furnished rooms, where the only decorations are altars with statues of Saint Peter and pictures of Jesus with rosaries, and candles. I ask questions about change, about how life used to be, and about what is different now. Many of the elders talk to me from behind glazed eyes, blurred with uncertainty, confused by the change happening so fast, by their inability to understand the language of their sons and daughters, saddened by the memories of the past, traumatized by the horrors of violence. In many of the interviews, my subjects blink constantly, and hold back their tears.

I see confusion in the eyes of an *anciano* (who asks me to conceal his identity) when he tells me about how for most of his life, he planted, harvested, and worked maguey, and left his home at 3 a.m. to walk to market to sell the ropes he had made. He laughs softly when he tells me about how he was robbed one day by bandits, and had to walk all the way home with nothing. He sighs when he tells me about how everything started to change in the 1970s, when the Chinese arrived, selling colored threads. This change gave people the possibility to add colorful stripes to their clothing for the first time, now distinguishing them as someone with more wealth than others. No longer did everyone have the unity that came with wearing the same white, undecorated tunics.

"We used to help each other," he says. If someone needed to build a house, everyone would come together and build the house in one day, but when the clothing changed, that sense of community ended." From that time onward, he adds, not only did clothing become more varied and colorful, but it opened the town to the world economy with the introduction of paper money. In coming years, the youth would begin to use new styles, while the elders continued to cling to what they knew.

"Their ideas did not change," he says. "They were still Mayas." However, when people started leaving San Pedro to look for work in other towns, or in the capital, or to join the military, they came back different. They used American pants, and refused to put on their *traje*. "When they tried to stop being Maya, that was when people started following that example. They used to stop and kiss *ancianos* on the hand as a sign of respect, but now there are many who do not do this." For teenagers, it became cool to rebel against *traje* and the Mayan traditions. "Young men who wore *traje* were teased, and the same with women. They felt insulted. They were made fun of and called names. But when they stopped wearing *traje*, they didn't even dress nicely. They didn't even tuck their shirts in!" He laughs and throws his hands into the air.

Then, he talks about the 80s, and *la violencia,* and his

voice goes soft, like he is afraid of someone overhearing. "The first people kidnapped, the first victims, were offered a deal. If they did not take it, the next day, they disappeared. It was a time of panic. We had to remain silent. After 5 p.m., everything was silent. Everyone in their homes. If someone spoke or gave information, they were killed. There was not light, and it was prohibited to light candles. If people wore clothing from Sololá or another department, we did not trust them, because we did not recognize them. The people in charge [the military] asked us to do favors for them, like we were slaves. If they did not do it, they were taken and never seen again. They went into the lake and never came out. They raped the women. They surprised us in the fields and we were afraid to go to work. Every time something happened, the church bells were rung as a warning to the rest of us. There were people from San Pedro who were responsible for many disappearances," he lowers his voice further. "There was a war between the two families. It was the _____ family who were responsible." He whispers a name that I have heard many times. "They had a deep hole on the lakeshore, where they threw people, still alive. There." He points on a map to where this hole was. I look at where his finger rests, and realize that it is just in front of where my house, Casa Shag, is now. They buried people alive, right where I sit on the rocks and contemplate the Lake, and how the *Xocomil* wind makes San Pedro seem restless and haunted.

He changes the subject and tells me about how tourism came to Lake Atitlán, and brought change with it faster than ever. He shows me his sunglasses. "We never had these before," he says, laughing. "And now we have many drugs, too. Many of our young people are getting lost and they are forgetting about what it means to be Mayan. That is why we have ceremonies and we try to remind them of their ancestors and the important traditions on important days like [Independence Day] and the Day of San Pedro."

"What is the most important tradition to the Tz'utujiil people today?" I ask him.

"It is the relationship between the community, nature, and the cosmic realm" he says. He tells me about Aajaaw, the god of the harvest, rains, and nature. "We must ask permission from Aajaaw before planting. We invoke Aajaaw when we need to ask for or give thanks for something. We ask El Pixaab' for permission before we get married or have children. We are constantly praying to the gods of nature for everything, everyday. For our sustenance. For our life. Without them, we cannot exist."

When Independence Day comes, the town is alive and sparkling with energy. Canons start booming at sunrise, the Evangelical school band has a 6 a.m. practice, and as I sit on the porch drinking coffee, I watch as everyone in town comes down to the lakeshore to bathe. Fireworks are constant throughout the morning, and children are running down pathways, laughing, squealing, and joyous.

At the parade, in the town center, tourists and locals line the streets together, and it is okay for me to have my camera out and to take pictures of everything. The streets are decorated with Guatemalan flags and blue and white streamers, and *everyone* is wearing traditional dress or another costume. As the parade passes by, there are marimba bands, and the honking brass of the Evangelical school, and dancers, and toddlers dressed up as suns, moons, flowers, and chickens. The last and largest group in the parade is a cluster of teens and young adults, marching with their faces covered by bandanas and masks, banding together in solidarity against oppression, waving signs that fault the police, the military, the government. Some have signs that plead to preserve San Pedro culture. Some tell stories of atrocities committed by authorities. Others read, "shouldn't independence mean freedom?"

The procession winds through town, ending in the high school basketball court in the market plaza, next to the Catholic Church. There is a grand stage set up, and a band with electric guitars and a drumset is playing Christian songs. The plaza fills with people. Everyone tries to fit, and it means a lot of squeezing and pushing, and climbing up onto balconies or roofs. People wave Guatemala flags, and carry painted banners that show pride in San Pedro. When the band plays the National Anthem, everyone in the crowd sings together. I climb onto the stage to get a shot and what I see is raw patriotism, *patria*. There are hands over hearts, eyes squeezed shut, hands in the air, bodies swaying to the rhythm. I see people brought to their knees. Brought to tears. When the song finishes, there is one moment of pure stillness. Then a canon shot. Then the crowd erupts in a mighty cheer.

As I watch, I can't help but wonder if these people understand how little their country has done for them.

After the parade, I am invited into the home of an old woman named Catarina Chavajay, who tells me about the lives of Tz'utujiil women. "Women in this community stay together," she begins. "Where you find one, there are probably more around." She talks about helping her father in the fields, carrying wool, but mostly she talks about weaving, and about the other work she did in the home. "I spent a lot of time grinding. Coffee had to be ground on a stone. Cacao had to be ground, and then we had to put fire under the stone to extract the juice. And I grind a lot of corn. *Ixtamal* is sacred to our people. It is where we come from, and it is what sustains us."

The home is tiny by American standards. It is one room, with a dirt floor, about 15 feet square, and has one window, without glass. In the corner is a wood-fired stove, where she cooks, and next to it is a small wooden shelf with a pot and a can of Nido, dehydrated milk. The only other items in her home are a mortar and pestle that sit in the middle of the floor. Next to them is a bowl of corn, soaking in water. "Sometimes our husbands have to very early to walk to the market, so we have to get up earlier to make their tortillas. Do you know how to make tortillas?"

I shake my head.

"Come *m'ija*." She takes my hand and pulls me gently to the ground. Her skin is soft, like worn leather. "Sit here. I will show you." She scoops up some of the corn kernels and sprinkles them onto the grinding stone. "Like this," she says, and begins tapping and rolling the pestle across them, creating a yellow mash. She hands me the pestle. "You try," she says.

I take the heavy cylinder from her and position myself on my knees in front of the grinding stone. She puts more corn down, and I try, clumsily rolling and tapping. Bits of corn fly off the mortar, I crush one of my fingers, and Catarina and the translator erupt with laughter. I smile and try again. But, like the weaving, this takes a remarkable amount of abdominal and upper arm strength that I seem to lack, as well as the ability to kneel comfortably. "You do it," I say gently, handing the pestle back to her.

Once the corn is ground, it is called *masa*. Sprinking some water on it forms a thick, yellow dough that can be shaped and molded. She takes a portion of this dough between her hands, rolls it into a ball, and begins clapping it back and forth. It is a soft, rhythmic sound I have heard every morning since my arrival. After a few moments, a perfect, round tortilla takes shape in her palm. She hands me some dough and encourages me to try. I create an amorphous lump, and again everyone laughs at me.

She lights the fire in her wood stove, and cooks the tortillas on a flat metal sheet. She fusses over my lumpy tortilla, and giggles like a child when she presents it to me, cooked and ready to eat. As I take my first bite, she and the translator congratulate me and applaud. "You are always welcome to come and make tortillas here, *niña,*"

Catarina says, hugging me.

As I leave, I thank her, promise her a copy of the photos I have taken, and make sure to show the traditional sign of respect by kissing her hand.

When I come back down the hill, the cultural differences between the Mayans and the rest of us are bigger than ever. I arrive at the veranda, and find Sid, and Cheryl yelling at each other in the lettuce garden.

"This is a Christian house." Sid shouts, two inches from her face. "You're a heathen! You can't talk like that here."

"Jesus fucking Christ," Cheryl says, turning to leave. "You're fucking delusional." She flips her long silver hair and slams through the gate. "Back in Alaska, people are crazy," she says to me, "but at least they have some fucking manners." She strolls away as though she is trying to make it obvious that Sid doesn't upset her.

"What was that about?" I ask him.

"She's a Satanist cunt," Sid says. "And I don't have to stand for that here."

"Not believing in God doesn't make someone a Satanist," I say.

"Look. I don't mind your phase of religious exploration," he says, and adds that everyone is entitled to their opinion, but "Cheryl better keep her goddamn mouth shut. If you're going to take her side, then you can just leave."

"Hey, I'm just an observer," I say, smiling. "That makes me neutral." From an anthropological perspective, Sid is a new breed of "Christian" to me – pot smoking, pot-bellied, drinking before breakfast, taking the Lord's name in vein, and using the c-word.

There are some other foreign Christians in town right now, the type with which I am more familiar. Their mission group is called *Proyecto Fe* (Project Faith), and they have been here with the Protestant church, doing "service work" for about a week now. They get together in the evenings for dinner at the Villa Sol hotel, and from our house I can hear them singing Christian camp songs that I used to know. Even though I know the words, I resist the urge to sing along.

"I think it actually takes more conviction to be an atheist," I say to Amber that evening as we walk together to the bar.

"What do you mean?" she says.

Up ahead of us, a man wearing a blue *Proyecto Fe* t-shirt slows down and cocks his head to listen.

"I mean, sometimes it's all kind of empty and terrifying when you don't believe in God," I say.

"Really?" Amber says. "I've never experienced that. Maybe it's just because I was just never raised to rely on it."

"Well, I was. My whole life, every time I got scared, I prayed. Now I suddenly feel like I'm not allowed to, and I don't know how to cope with even the simplest things anymore." I look out across the lake where a red moon is rising and feel a chill go down my back.

Amber follows my gaze. "Red sky at night, sailor's delight. Red sky in the morning, sailors take warning."

The man with the *Proyecto Fe* shirt stops to read the menu outside of Tin Tin Restaurant. "Have you eaten here?" he says as we walk past.

"Yeah," I say. "It's some of the best food in town. I eat here all the time."

"You know," he says, reaching out and stopping us. "I couldn't help but overhear your conversation."

"Okay," Amber says. "What do *you* think?"

"Well, I'm with *Proyecto Fe*, and we're here in town working with the kids, teaching a bible school and doing some construction projects. I'm a Christian, and I believe that Jesus Christ was sent to earth as our savior, and I have dedicated my life to sharing His word and spreading His love."

Amber and I stare at him.

"Um, congratulations," I stammer, and Amber yanks me away, suppressing giggles.

"My name is Bill," he shouts after us. "Come by the Villa Sol Hotel if you want to talk. I can help. We'll be here until the end of the week."

"We're totally going to hell," I say, still laughing, as we duck into the bar.

Inside, we order drinks and I tell Amber how crazy it seems to me that I used to really believe all that "religious mumbo-jumbo".

Next to us, Cheryl is working on two drinks simultaneously. She rolls her eyes and sighs. "It's all a bunch of bullshit," she says, tapping the ash off her cigarette.

"True dat," Amber says.

Cheryl leans onto the bar and opens her eyes wide and looks at us very seriously. "Where I come from, if someone comes into your room in the middle of the night, and shines a light in your face, it's rape."

"What?" I say.

"Where I come from, if someone comes into your room and says, 'You're going to have my baby,' and shines a big fucking light in your face, it's rape," she repeats. The bar falls silent. "He didn't give Mary any choice. He just came down and said, 'you're going to have my baby.' Goddamn. I mean, come on. She was fucking raped."

"God as a rapist," I say. "Now that is something I have never even considered."

"Think about it," Cheryl says, shooting one whisky, then the other, and standing to leave. "Whelp, I'm going to go home and roll a joint the size of my wrist." She stubs out her cigarette. "I think I can get it in my mouth."

On our way home later that night, Amber and I walk by the Villa Sol, where Bill and all the other members of *Proyecto Fé* are gathered in the *comedor*, sitting at long tables. I can't help but stop outside the door and listen. *You are my strength when I am weak. You are the treasure that I seek. You are my all in all. When I fall down you pick me up. When I am dry you fill my cup. You are my All in all. Jesus. Lamb of God. Holy is your name. Jesus. Lamb of God. Holy is your name.*

Amber squeezes her arms around my waist. "Be strong, Cindy," she says, poking me in the side. "Stay away from the light."

"Shut up," I say, laughing and shoving her away. It hurts because part of me still wants to be 13 years old again, sitting in that warm Costa Rican kitchen, with Doña Flora peeling vegetables, stoking the wood fire in the oven, washing dishes with soft wrinkled hands, smelling onions and garlic and black beans, and listening to the sizzling oil and the VIM group singing. Inside the Villa Sol, I see at least thirty people, sitting close together, all of them singing like I used to sing. Even the teenage boys, who anywhere else would think they were too cool to sing like that, are belting it out. I used to squeeze my eyes shut just like them, and hold my hands up in the air, because that's what people did when they felt truly moved by the Spirit.

I realize that it is slowly getting easier not to believe—like I am settling into being an atheist. By doing this, I have been able to step back from everything I was brainwashed with as a kid, and am finally starting to trust what I see with my own eyes, and what I feel in my gut. As twisted around as I am with all the drugs and drinking, and the feeling of having fallen out of grace, there is one thing I know for sure. Christianity is not the answer. It is just an easy way out.

A few days later, Elena stops by San Pedro before going back to the States, and I tell her all about the drugs, and the wind, and my steamy evening with Christopher, who I haven't seen since despite my nightly strolls from bar to bar. Within a day she finds a boyfriend, named Jay, who has a girlfriend back home in England, but agrees that fooling around with Elena is okay, as long as they don't have sex.

To celebrate, we buy three space cookies from Dave and each eat half of one, waiting to see what it will do before we eat the other half. Within an hour, Elena and Jay are rolling around on the bed laughing like crazy, but nothing is happening to me. So I eat the other half of mine. And then I eat Elena's other half. We hit the town, laughing at nothing, rowdy, and stumbling, and find ourselves ordering food at Tin Tin, even though no one is really hungry. I am starting to feel squinty and wobbly, like my head is a giant hot-air-balloon and my body is the size of an ant.

"It's hard to balance on these tiny legs," I stammer, peering down at my distant feet. I try to sit in the chair, but it is so tiny that I have trouble finding it.

"I feel like a puddle," Elena says, smooshing herself into Jay.

Jay stands up and unscrews the light bulb over our table. "It's too challenging," he says.

My ears are ringing and I get the spins. The thatched roof over our heads spins over me, like a 1950s UFO. "They should be careful with this thing," I say. "We're going to punch through the atmosphere." I am weightless and the world around me is like a huge canvas painting. The sky hangs precariously over our heads like it is all about to collapse inwards.

Too much. This is too much.

The spins become worse, and when the food arrives, it looks like worms, crawling. The smell of curry makes me dizzy. The smell of it is like someone has put mud in my mouth. It is hard to focus my eyes enough to pick up my fork.

Just as I manage to take my first bite, and dribble it onto my shirt, Christopher strolls into the restaurant.

"That's the guy," I say, perking up and nudging Elena. "He's a *doctor.*"

"Cute," she says.

"Chris!" I shout. He waves. "Come and join us!"

He pulls over a chair and squeezes in at the table, looks deep into my eyes, just like before, and asks me how my project is going.

"Um, good," I say. I rock backwards and push my food away. I am starting to feel sick. I want to respond to him and sound intelligent, but I can't get my brain to connect with my lips. "I'll be honest with you," I mutter eventually. "We had some space cookies before we came here and I'm really fucked up."

"Awesome," he says, but his smile falls. In his eyes I see unmistakable disappointment. The look says, *I though she was cool, but she's just another drugged-up hippie.*

I want to crawl into the bathroom and puke, and eventually, that's what I do, kneeling on the cement floor with my head hanging down into the toilet bowl, crying and heaving for what seems like hours. I throw up the entire contents of my stomach, then curl up in the fetal position facing the wall, and sob. I feel poisoned. Sad. Violated. Empty, like something was stolen. Eventually Elena and Jay knock on the door and I manage to unlock it so they can help me to my feet and walk me home.

The next morning we decide the cookies were laced with opium. After Elena leaves for her flight, I spend the better part of the afternoon running all over town looking for Christopher, desperate to explain to him that I am not a druggie like everyone else here. That I *do* have substance, and he was right to look at me the way he did. But I can't find him anywhere. After that night, I never see him again.

Once the moon is waning, things go back to normal in our house, with Amber, Cathy and I doing cocaine and drinking every night. We sleep until early afternoon every day, and when we all finally get up, Amber makes us "cowboy coffee" with the grounds swimming around in the cup.

I still check in on Kayla and take her to Solar Pools

for baths, and one day while I am walking up the stairs in my bathing suit, I meet a man, named Jeff, who smiles at me and offers me his towel. Phil takes Kayla home and I sit with Jeff and have coffee. He tells me that he has just climbed Volcán Pacaya. "You should have seen it," he says, glowing with excitement. "All the greens and yellows. It was pretty awesome."

"I climbed it," I say. "But I never made it to the crater." Then I tell him all about Paul and the lightning and pump him with questions. Did he go in the morning or afternoon? Did anyone mention lightning? Did the tour operators seem concerned about safety?

"Nah, our trip was fine. You should go back up there someday," he says. "It's really an amazing place."

I nod. "Maybe I will," I say and I invite him to stop by our house that night. "We're having a party. It should be a good time."

Jeff shows up with a gram of coke and Amber and Cathy like him right away. They keep nudging us together, and arranging themselves so Jeff and I are forced to sit practically on top of each other. Before I know what is really happening, my legs are draped across his lap and his hand is working its way up under the leg of my pants. An hour later, we are in my bedroom and he is literally tearing my clothes off. He does it so passionately it is almost violent. So violently, it is almost scary. Once we are naked, we each do more lines of coke, and suddenly I know what Amber and Cathy are talking about. I am completely uninhibited. I don't care whether his hand brushes across the rolls of fat on my stomach, or if he can feel my stretch marks. I don't even think about Christopher. I just let it happen. Outside, our dogs bark like crazy.

The next morning when I wake up, Jeff is gone. But he shows up at the door that afternoon with a timid look on his face. "This girl I was hooking up with in Xela showed up here, and I think I'm going to go with her to Antigua. But I had a lot of fun last night. I wanted you to know that. It was great."

"Yeah, it was," I say, knowing I have to be graceful. So I reach up and brush my hand across his cheek, and kiss him gently. "Safe travels," I say, smiling.

It is my first true one-night stand.

The next Thursday afternoon, I bring Kayla to our house after Solar Pools, and sit with her on the couch, feeding her eggs, with her brown eyes rolling back in her head.

As soon as Cathy and Amber come home, they are in love with her. Cathy tickles her chin while Amber eases a brush through her hair. And Kayla smiles for the longest period of time I have ever seen. The puppies lick her toes, and she giggles, just like a normal happy kid. As the shadows began to stretch thin and orange across the red tile floor, Moises, our Tz'utujiil landlord, pops his head through the door to let us know the water tank is full, and his eyes fall on Kayla's face.

"Ahhh," he says softly, pulling his hat from his head and placing it over his chest. *"Tan preciosa.* What is her name?"

"Se llama Kayla," I say, watching in admiration. He is such a weathered and gentle man, reminding me of someone who once had a serious substance abuse problem and has spent all his Wednesday evenings in the back rows of AA meetings, never saying a word. As he kneels down beside the sofa, he takes her hand, and begins stroking her cheek softly with the side of his thumb.

"Pobrecita," he says, rising to his feet and placing his hat back on his head. When he leaves, I follow him out into the garden.

"It is good of you to care for her," he says, shaking my hand with pride. "She is a very special little girl. She deserves all the love you can give her."

"Yes," I say softly. "She does. Her parents have trouble knowing how to care for her."

"It can be hard sometimes for people to take care of many children. I have problems myself with only four of them. I sometimes make only 15 Quetzales a day, and it is hard to feed hungry children with so little money. They have been hungry before, and I do everything I can for them. But somehow, God always seems to provide for us."

I take Kayla home to her parents and her father, Reuben takes her into his arms with care. Each time I see him with her, there seems to be a little bit more tenderness in his touch than the time before—like he is finally learning after all these years, how to love her. Maybe I am helping him to see how precious she is. Maybe I am making a difference.

That evening, just as Amber, Cathy, and I sit down to gorge ourselves on spaghetti and red wine, Moisés appears again in the doorway clutching his hat and looking timid and forlorn.

"Pardon the intrusion," he says, bowing slightly. "I know it isn't very much, but I wanted to give this for Kayla." He pulls a five-Quetzal bill from his wallet, and puts it into my hand. "I don't know what you will do with it, but I hope it will help."

"Thank you, Moises. I'm sure her family will appreciate it." I take his hand and shake it firmly, placing my left hand over his knuckles. And then like an old habit, I say, God bless you, "*Diós te bendiga*," before I can catch myself.

He tilts his head and smiles at me, and backs hastily through the door.

"Perhaps there is still some good in the world," Cathy says, slathering butter onto a piece of bread.

"It was almost like he was scared to come in here. Did you guys notice that?" I say.

"Maybe it's because the Smoking Jesus is uncovered," Amber says with her mouth full.

I turn my head and look behind me to see the Smoking Jesus staring down at us with a half-smoked joint sticking out of the hole. "My god," I say, feeling His eyes dart towards me. "That must have terrified him."

ICE-COLD CRYSTAL

"La noche anda con su secreto. La noche anda con su gracia. La noche tiene quien la cuida. Por eso, no hay que intentar hacer lo malo. La noche tan obscura no nos pertenece a los seres humanos."

"The night has secrets. The night comes with grace. The night has its keepers. For this reason none should do wrong. The night so dark does not belong to humans."

-Tz'utujiil Oral Tradition
La Abuela Luna y Otras Historias del Cielo

Las Piramides has a little shop that sells incense, teas, herbs, and crystals. One day I am browsing and my hand passes over a bowl of rocks, and lights up with a sensation of heat.

"It's talking to you," the woman at the counter says, noticing the surprise on my face. "Crystals are very powerful," she says. "That one is amethyst, good for dreams. It has attractive properties."

I'm not sure what this means, but the heat from the rock is unmistakable, so I buy it. Back at our house, Amber lights up when she sees it and uses it as a fortune-telling pendulum. When she asks it questions, it spins one

151

way for yes, and the other way for no. The crystal tells Amber that soon she will find the love of her life and have a large family; it tells Cathy that she will make a great fortune; and it tells me that I will survive Guatemala, and that I will make it home again.

I carry the crystal in my pocket. It is hot against my leg, and almost seems to make people kinder and more interested in talking to me. It is warm and strong after yoga, when I'm balanced, warmer when I sit on the rocks at the lakeshore and ground myself, and warmest when I am truly *in tune* with the rhythms of the earth. When I am high on cocaine, it turns ice cold.

I start to use the crystal as a toy for foreplay, dragging it along arms and legs and chests, giving men chills because there is actually something to it. It is fascinating to me to discover how different men's bodies can be from each other, and how differently they act in bed. Some are sensual and sincere in their touches and teach me something new every time they climax. Some are just rough and ready and full of animal energy and come without warning, howling along with the dogs in the streets. All of them make me feel good. And as they pass through town one by one, I start to slowly learn how to let go of the idea of loving them, and to just enjoy the way two bodies sliding together in the darkness feels. That pure, simple, primal urge surges through me and I let it surge through each one of my lovers, making sure they will never forget their nights with me after they are gone.

Amber has finally introduced me to Rosa, and I am buying my own coke now. One afternoon I go in and Rosa isn't home, but her seven-year-old daughter comes up to me and says, "*que quieres?*" What do you want?

I hesitate. "*Una grama,*" I say.

"*Momento.*" She disappears into a back room and reappears a moment later with a little baggie full of white powder.

As I walk away, I realize that I've just bought cocaine

from a seven-year-old girl.

I hardly ever sleep at night anymore, except in fits and spurts, with my mouth dried out and my head resting in the armpit of whoever takes me home. After the long nights of sex and heavy drinking, I watch the San Pedro mornings from the other side of sleeplessness, like they are the end instead of the beginning. They dawn blue and orange, with the lake like glass, and extra volcanoes on the horizon. In the mornings, when I am walking home, my underwear stuffed into my bag, and my head hazy with uncertainty about what I've done all night, there are never any clouds in the sky. Only the crowing of roosters, the tapping of pestles, and sometimes the sound of Mayan chanting.

If I catch it right, I can watch the sunrise before I go to sleep—that big, flaming ball, slinking up over the lake, making spider webs and dewdrops glisten. I see men on their way to the lakeshore with towels over their shoulders, women with tubs of laundry balanced on their heads, and the first *lancha*, breaking the water, heading for Pana. I can see my breath. It swirls up away from me, like my life. Spiraling. Spinning. Out of control.

By the end of October, the allure of sex grows stale. I find myself pouring so much energy into it that I have nothing left for myself at the end. While my lovers tell me that I recharge them, they must be stealing my energy, because they leave me feeling drained and helpless, even if I haven't done any of the work.

Before I know it, I have just over three weeks left in San Pedro, and my body is wrecked. I am completely and totally exhausted, and it is a tired that rests deep inside me—more than something that can be fixed by a good night's sleep. My legs are always like jelly even if I haven't had sex in days. My nose has forgotten how to breathe clean and easy, and I am starting to really hate the way coke makes me feel the next day after I've had too much, with my sinuses hollowed out and raw, and my entire body crying and cramping up because I'm not drinking enough water.

By now I am so firmly entrenched in the San Pedro drug scene that I have become friends with Helen, a hustler from the Capital, who happens to have the cleanest coke in town. One evening I am at Barrio drinking rum while she flirts with men in five different languages, and sorts out lines of coke right there on the counter in front of everyone.

"Cindy, do you want a line?" she asks me, in her sexy, sleazy Guatemalan way. Her slim legs are crossed, and her shimmering flip flops hang down off her dark feet in a sexy way, making me almost envy her. I shrug and wander over. Snorting it right at the bar seems to be a step up from doing lines off the back of the toilet, secretly, shamefully, divvying it up with my driver's license and snorting it through my crispest 100Q bill, rolled tight into a straw. She pulls a key out of her bag and hands it to me carefully, with a lump of white on the tip. I sniff in and feel the familiar speeding up of my heartbeat, and the high turns to a gentle shake in my bones and a tingling in my pelvis. I clean my nose, careful to make sure no white clumps are sticking to my nose hairs, and start dancing to the music.

"Cindy," Helen says a moment later. "Davíd keeps asking about you. He's so cute. You should go for it."

Just the thought of it makes me feel exhausted. "I don't care if he's cute. I'm getting tired of all this meaningless sex. I need to just get a couple of nights of rest. I feel like crap."

"Oh, come on. I bet he can make you feel *good*," she says, drawing out the vowels. "Besides, how can you ever be tired of sex?"

"Not sex in general. Just the meaningless kind. I'm sick of all these boys who come breezing through town and only pay attention to me because they want to get laid. It's just a distraction."

"From what? What else do you have to do?"

My Fulbright? I don't say it out loud, but the twinge of guilt courses through me as I think about what a delinquent Fulbright scholar I am, sitting here in bars, night after night, snorting coke off a key, making friends with a hustler. With only three weeks left, I can't help but feel that I have not done much true anthropology here.

Davíd, who I met a few minutes earlier when I dropped my drink on the floor, comes over and pushes Helen out of the way, wraps his arms around my waist and tries to kiss me. I pull back, laughing, and look at him. She is right. He is very cute—adorable actually—with a dark, chiseled face, blue eyes, and curly brown hair. He is very European. I am crazy to resist him.

"I do not have a bed to sleep in," he says in a thick French accent. "I can come to your house? I can sleep with you?"

"Hah!" I scoff. "Good line. Right to the point. Why don't you have a bed?" My smile probably leads him on more, but I can't help it.

"My roommate went back with a girlfriend. They were kissing. I cannot disturb them."

"So you were sexiled," I say, remembering the phrase from college.

"What is mean, sexiled?" He tries to kiss me again and I pull away. "I do not understand. Why you not want me? I am *French*."

I roll my eyes. "I don't care what you are. You can't sleep with me. I need some rest. I haven't slept in days."

"Okay, fine. You win. But at least you will let me kiss you." He catches me off guard and plants one on me. I laugh and accept it, then get up and walk back to the pool table. I flop back against the wall to watch the game, and see him staring at me from where I left him. He throws me a disappointed, pleading look. I smile and shake my head, and wave at him. My head is spinning. I am totally drunk. It is 4:00 in the morning when I stumble home alone after a whole night of playing hard-to-get.

At Casa Shag, I collapse into bed without peeing, changing, or brushing my teeth. I stare at the bottle of water across the room, desperately thirsty but not wanting to move. I think about witchcraft, and I squint my eyes in serious concentration, and try to move the bottle with my mind. It doesn't budge. With my last reserves of energy, I heave myself up and chug the whole thing. Then I pass out and sleep until late the next afternoon.

When I wake up. I want to go right back to sleep and stay that way until my Fulbright is over. I check the countdown in my journal. Nineteen more days. In it I write:

I am looking forward to quiet nights and quiet mornings. Waking up in a quiet room, with the gentle hum of an air conditioner instead of roosters and barking dogs and marching bands and shouting. I am looking forward to cleansing myself. To not feeling drunk and hung over and with my body always totally spent. I am looking forward to going to bed early, at nine or ten, without some random French guy trying to follow me home. Cable television and refrigerators and vending machines that sell diet coke. Drinking water from the tap. I am looking forward to grocery shopping. Bathtubs. Flying down the road in my car with the windows down, singing at the top of my lungs with no one there to judge me or ask nosy stupid questions about where I'm from or how long I've been traveling or what I'm doing here. Driving forever into the night. Stopping to pump my own gas when I run out. Walking into a place where no one knows my name.

I suppose there are things here I will miss. Sunrise over the lake. The coldness of the water. Papaya. Pineapple. The parties. Fly by night friends and random lovers. Lawlessness. Unending freedom.

One afternoon a few days later, I drop acid. An hour later, I am sitting on the floor in Barrio, tripping, with the music thumping in my ears. I am captivated by patterns I see in the golden fur of a dog that has wandered over and is lying in my lap, and I look up at everyone, way up high on their barstools, towering above me, and think, *What am I doing down here on the floor?* It doesn't matter. For a precious moment, I love everything about my life. Even Guatemala.

Later, just as I am starting to come down, I meet Sven. He is one of those rugged, mysterious men, with three-day scruff and dark features, and a face and body that looks more like a man than a grown-up boy. He seems like a character from a mystery novel. A suspect. At first, I am attracted to his thick Russian accent, and I think, *well, I've slept with a Lars, a Niels, and a Shlomi. How cool would it be to sleep with a guy named Sven before I go?* So out of habit, I climb onto the stool next to him, and order another drink.

I don't feel like explaining the Fulbright, so I lie when he asks me what I am doing in San Pedro. "I've been living here for a while, just traveling. But I'm going home soon."

"Where's home?" he says. *Very home?* My blood tingles and I get excited by the accent.

"The States," I say.

"Why the *hell* you want to go there?"

I laugh a little, and fight off a sense of annoyance. There is no way I can explain to him how badly I need to leave this country. It is definitely time to go.

"Why don't you just keep traveling?" Sven says.

"Because I'm out of money. Why? Do you have money for me?" I laugh and punch his arm to show I am joking.

But he lurches back from me. "I am offended that you say this. Women always coming to me for my money." He gets up, shoves the bar stool away and disappears.

Later that night, after Barrio closes, Sid and I buy a gallon of rum and a two-liter of Coca-cola and go to his veranda for drunken singing. I break into Patsy Cline, and am loving it, totally in my element, finally singing my heart out, forgetting completely about my stage fright, and singing just to sing. Suddenly there are a dozen people there, all of us drunk, singing like sailors, not caring how much noise we make. We go through *Country Roads* and *You are my Sunshine*, and *I'll Fly Away*, and just as I start into *Bobby McGee*, Sven comes strolling through the gate.

Without asking, he makes himself a Cuba and pulls up a chair. I ignore him and sing the second verse, and the chorus again, then I break into the la-la-la bit with so much soul I nearly erupt into tears. I use my whole body to sing like Janis, letting myself flail all over the place, not caring. And I finish and am out of breath and jubilant, and the night air feels cooler and fresher around me and everyone is clapping, except for Sven.

"Why don't you just shut up?" he says. "You are not an artist. I mean, can't we just have some silence?"

We all sit for a moment, stunned.

"Fuck you," I say, feeling the rage build up inside of me, and the heat burn in my face. *How dare this man come in here,* I think, *to this place that has been my home longer than it has been his. To Sid's Veranda. The land of debauchery and drunken singing.* "If you want silence, maybe you should go somewhere else."

"Amen girl," someone says. But the leftover LSD is twisting my mind around and I don't really hear it. *My singing sucks. I'm not beautiful.* I reach in my pocket for the crystal and it is icy, colder than cold.

"Are you kicking me out?" Sven says.

It isn't my house either, and I have no right to kick him out, even though I wish I could and Sid probably won't object. "All I'm saying is that you're the one who should shut up, you arrogant asshole." The sound of my voice coming out so angrily startles me. Tears stream down my face and I am thankful for the darkness, hoping maybe no one will see them. I want to throw my drink at him. I want the glass to smash and leave a big bloody gash on his forehead. I know I won't miss. I want to push him over backwards in his chair so that he falls into the yard and his legs go up over his head.

Next to me, someone starts humming something.

"Shhh," I say, sarcastically. "We want silence here. No humming." I turn to Sven. "What right do you have to come in here and tell me or anyone else to shut up? You bastard." Then again, what right did any of us have to be there, parading around like San Pedro is our home, when all we did was steal it from the Mayans?

"Well, with you singing like that, you are just wanting people to notice you. You are throwing yourself all over the place for attention."

"Do you think that's why I sing? To be noticed? I sing to sing, because it makes me feel free. Because I love to sing. Not for you or anyone else to notice me. So don't presume to know so much about who I am. You have no clue."

People are laughing, like this is fun for them. Meanwhile I am welling with hatred for all of them, and I yell at Sven intermittently for half an hour, until finally he says, "Girl, you will give me nightmares for a month."

I stop talking for a while and try to control the come-down from my trip. The acid has mostly faded, but the silent tears are still rolling down my cheeks. The way I see it, telling me to stop singing is like telling a mother her baby is ugly. It cuts me to the core. Someone asks me to sing something else, and tugs on my sleeve. "No," I say. "I'm not singing any more tonight. Not in front of that self-righteous shithead." I point to Sven and he rolls his eyes.

After that, it is like an endurance trial between Sven and me, and I know that neither one of us wants to leave first, because doing so is like admitting defeat.

"This morning I was reading in a restaurant," Sven says to someone else, "and I just wanted some quiet, and over the wall I hear a man whistling. And not just whistling, but whistling like a goddamn artist. And I want to scream at him to tell him to shut up. I just want some quiet, and there he is thinking he is so great—"

"Like a goddamn artist?" I say, interrupting. "What is art? Aren't we all artists? Does it matter whether anyone's listening? Can't we just sing or whistle or do art for art's sake, because we like it. People are happy and that's what bothers you. And this is their home. You can't just come into a town and tell the people that live there to shut up so *you* can have some peace."

I realize that this is the last word, so I down the rest of my drink and stand to leave. "Goodnight," I say, slamming the gate behind me.

As I head towards our house, I pick up a piece of firewood to carry like a club, just in case the dogs sense my rage and decide to attack.

MACHETE GATHERING

"Que nadie esté hablando, porque Dios está moviendo el planeta, seguramente en algo le estamos fallando porque ya está llamando la atención. Ooh, Sublime Dios que ha movido nuevamente el mundo."

"No one should speak [during an earthquake], because God is moving the planet, surely in something we have failed it because it is trying to get our attention. Ooh, Sublime God, that has moved again this world."

-Tz'utujiil Oral Tradition
La Abuela Luna y Otras Historias del Cielo

During my last San Pedro full moon, I go to the psychedelic gathering in a van driven by a man with no legs. The trance music pounds out over the lagoon and I sneak in without paying the cover charge because I know the guy at the gate. Down on the beach, lights are flashing everywhere, and people are dancing like maniacs and twirling various flaming things. Most are naked from the waist up, and covered in sweat. Others are huddled together under blankets because the temperature has dropped enough that we can see our breath.

I find some folks I know sitting cross-legged in a circle, rolling a joint under a thatched *palapa*. I join them and offer up my baggie of coke. Just as we finish our lines, the ground starts shaking underneath us. It rolls up and down like waves on the ocean. "Do you guys feel that?" I say.

"Look," someone say, pointing to the thatch on the roof that is shaking. Then there is no question about it. The ground lurches and some people standing nearby are thrown to their knees. Food slides off the tables and into the grass. The rumbling sounds like a freight train coming closer and the music down on the beach skips like a scratched CD. Then just as quickly as it came, the tremor dies away.

"Now watch," someone says. "The volcano's gonna blow. I had a dream about it the other night."

"Yeah right," I say. "That thing's been dormant for a thousand years." But I look up at it anyway and wonder if it is possible.

By the time the sun comes up I have snorted a record quantity of cocaine and am sitting alone on the beach in a daze, watching people dance and run naked into the water, throwing their hands up into the air and shouting "Jai-mah!" I have no idea what this means, but I know that my relationship with cocaine is over. I can't take anymore.

Somehow, I make my way back up to the road and hitch a pick-up back into town. As we ride past people on the streets, they glower at us and hold their machetes in front of them, menacingly. We are all sweaty, dirty, still high, and dazed. But we still get the message. The psychedelic gathering had kept the entire village awake all night because the music was so loud. *We are intruders.* Their looks are like daggers. They slice through me, saying *You aren't welcome here anymore.*

There are moments in life that decide things, events that divide time into before and after. The morning after the party was one of those, and back in town expats are referring to the party as the "machete gathering." That morning I knew that my relationship with drugs was over. For the rest of the day, the whole town is hung-over. Subdued. Silent. Like the relationship between us and the locals has changed for good. Like San Pedro is finally rejecting those who don't belong.

At our house I pack a small bag and head across the lake for San Marcos, determined to spend this last week in Guatemala cleansing and producing something comprehensive for my Fulbright, though I don't know what it will be. I've decided to disappear without warning, to fast and cleanse my body, and to hide away in a nice hotel room, alone. Not drinking. Not going out at night and flirting with guys. Not even smoking pot. Just writing. Finishing my Fulbright, cataloguing my pictures, organizing and analyzing my field notes, and just being sober.

I can't get out of town fast enough. On the way to the dock, I pass too many people I know and they all want to know where I am going with my pack, and how I am feeling after last night. Someone even asks me what I ate for breakfast. But the locals, who have always said "Hola, Cindy," or "Hola, Chac," just stare at me with judgment on their faces. I walk faster, imagining a shopping mall or a café back home where I can sit anonymously and do whatever I want, without anyone noticing or caring at all.

In San Marcos I rent a room at a boutique hotel on the water called Posada Shuman. When I crawl into the plush bed with crisp white sheets, I gasp and moan because of how good it feels compared to my scratchy foam bed and lumpy pillow in San Pedro. I sleep for a day and a half solid.

That week, I meditate every day. At dawn, I go to the pyramid for yoga and breathe deeply into my poses. After three days of eating nothing at all, I go to the market and buy pineapple, tomato, and cucumber, and I eat just produce until the week is over. At sunset, I sit on the dock and watch San Pedro across the water. I try to process everything that's happened. The town is so small in the shadow of that volcano, but even from here, 13 kilometers away, I can feel its pulse, throbbing with the energy of collision.

On the day before my flight to the States, I go back to San Pedro one last time, to finish packing everything. It doesn't take long, and that afternoon I sit with Cathy on the couch, painting the dogs' toenails again, and turning down the joint she passes me. We watch the rain come down in torrents. The doors are open, and we stare out into the garden, where the grass is drowning, and the trees bend under the weight of so much water. A cascade sweeps down over the porch in a solid sheet, and the red tile floor of the living room is splattered and slippery. The power is out and the world is dark, dancing gray-blue, as leaves twitch and huge buckets of rain hit the earth and splash back up into the sky.

Amber appears at the end of the garden, a hunched figure in a blue-tent poncho. Her steps are heavy and slow, like she is swimming through the rain instead of walking. She bursts into the house splashing water everywhere, and presents a dripping wet, cold liter of Gallo, and peels off her sopping raincoat. "Oy," she says. "That bloody thing doesn't work for shit. Let's get drunk."

She changes her clothes and squeezes in beside us on the couch. We drink out of plastic cups, and the beer hits my stomach like a lump of tar. I am quiet, because in two days I will see my family, who will welcome me with open arms, but they won't understand any of what has happened here, least of all my religious revelations. While I am totally ready to go home, I am not sure I am quite ready for them, or for what will happen next with my life or my ex-boyfriend. *Where will I live? What will I do? Will we get back together?*

"Everything will work out just like it's supposed to, Chickadee," Amber says.

"I know," I say. Though I don't really.

"So, who's going to get the next beer?" Cathy asks. We don't have a fridge, so going to get the beer means going up to Pedro's *tienda*. We are too impatient to wait for the rain to stop, so I change into shorts and a tank top and dash through the front doors barefoot and into the majesty of the rain. The ground is completely saturated and mud squishes between my toes. I shout and jump into puddles as I run down the path towards the *tienda*, where I grab the beer and run home, depositing it with Amber and Cathy.

Then, without refilling my cup, I run back outside, into the yard, and let the rain pour down over me. It streams down over my face and body, and I laugh and holler and whoop. I dance like something wild has awakened inside me, and grab fistfuls of mud, throwing them up into the air. I spin, and tumble, and twirl to the music of Atitlán, soaking, bathing in the wet earth, until the rain stops.

Back inside Amber hands me a towel and throws her arms around me. "You're a wild woman," she says. "I'm going to write about your mad-Guate rain dance in my book."

The next morning, Amber and Cathy go with me to the dock. While we wait for the *lancha* to fill up, we sit at D'Noz drinking coffee, leaning on each other and stroking each others' hair, the two of them taking turns saying that they can't believe I am leaving. "We're going to miss you so much," they both say.

"Me too," I say, even though I don't think I'll miss any of this, really. When the boat finally pulls away, I breathe a sigh of relief, realizing how suffocating the freedom of San Pedro can be.

I look up at the girls waving and see Cathy wiping

tears off her cheeks. Dean and Monique come out on the balcony of D'Noz, waving with Clodagh and Phil, and the banana bread women gather on the dock, and as I take my last look at San Pedro it seems like the whole town is waving to me. "Adiós, Cin-dee!" people shout. "Have a good trip. *Buen viaje.*"

"Where are you going?" the woman next to me on the boat asks.

"Home," I say, smiling. "To the States."

"Oh! I have a sister in Texas," she says. "Can you say hello to her for me?"

QUIET

Coming from Guatemala back into the U.S. is one last groggy high. I take a sleeping pill when I arrive at the airport, because I am ready for all this to be over and to help me rest on the plane. As soon as I am through the ticket line, it starts to kick in.

I wander through the airport shops in a dizzy haze, buying last-minute souvenirs. Coffee. Jade. Woven change purses and t-shirts with pictures of Tikal and monkeys and lizards. I consider some bumper stickers that said, "Yo (heart) Guatemala," but even though I want something for my car, I decide against them. I don't heart Guatemala. I don't even like Guatemala any more.

At security, entire families are draped over each other, kissing and hugging their sons before they go through the metal detector, with tears spilling down their faces. Watching them reminds me once again of how much trauma these people go through in their lives. For a family to send someone away, without knowing whether that person would ever come back is terrifying. It is a human sacrifice, giving up a family member for the hope of brighter things to come. On the traveler's side, getting a visa and being able to go to America legally is a tremendous process. In Guatemala, it involves waiting in line at the embassy for days, sometimes camping on the street for months, navigating bureaucracy and red tape, being patient, having to prove yourself over and over, being judged heavily, knowing how to read and write, being willing to fill out form, after form, after form, and leaving everything behind.

The sons who have gone through all this don't know what is out there, across the border; they only know the stories, and secretly they are terrified, though they do not show it to their mothers. They hope they can find work. They hope they don't get arrested, harassed, or accused of being a terrorist. They hope they can send some money home, even if it is just a little. In these last moments, the members of these families cling to each other, crying, grasping, trying to hold on, knowing that what is ahead will be so much different from what they knew before.

As I sit down at the gate, I feel more American already. Gone are the dirty feet and withered faces, and the stenches of urine and poverty. Instead, the shiny vinyl seats are filled with businessmen in pressed suits and polished shoes or snakeskin boots, reading the *Prensa Libre* and talking on cell phones, and women wearing too much make-up, with their hair dyed and styled crisply into place. The duty free shop nearby fills the air with strong perfumes, and the smell of packaging, chemicals, cardboard, and coffee.

With the sleeping pill in full effect, I wander onto the plane barely conscious, slip earplugs in and ignore all the safety information. The air in the cabin is sticky and hot, and everyone keeps reaching up to adjust the overhead fans. Outside, heat radiates off the tarmac and thick, afternoon clouds move in. I slide into sleep just after we take off. Once we pierce through the clouds, my eyes flutter open for a moment, and I catch one last hazy glimpse of Guatemala. To the west, the black tips of eleven volcanoes stretch across the sky, perfect triangles all in a row, poking up through a sea of wispy white.

In Miami, the terminal is so quiet and cold compared to the Guatemala City airport that it seems more appropriate to whisper, and the only sounds are muffled footsteps and the whir of dry air through the ceiling vents. Signs overhead point towards customs. *Aduana. Imigración.* Baggage claim. Gray carpet covers the walls and floors, florescent lights hum, and I slide silently down the corridor into the maze of ramps and long hallways.

In the customs bay, the gray silence and sterility is overwhelming—like a prison compared to Guatemala, without its heat and noise and color. The customs officials are stiff, starched, and institutional, like they might not even be people at all but realistic robots. They are frowning, pressed, and loaded down with belts holding tear gas, pepper spray, batons, cuffs, bullet clips and handguns. The shiny squeak of polished leather and the uniforms glistening with medals and merits are so different from the lazy, casual Guatemalan police, whose AK-47s were always draped over their shoulders more like purses than weapons. Looking around, I can't help but think about those who I saw hugging their families in Guatemala, who are coming to this country for the first time. There are no marimba bands or costumed dancers to welcome them. Will they bask in the quiet of it, like me, or will they feel empty, afraid, foreign, and lonely? Or is that the whole idea?

I move through the lines quickly, and clear immigration with no problems, just a moment of consideration, a stamp, and a mumbled "welcome home."

The highway is dark and empty. A light drizzle falls on the windshield and Dad puts the wipers on the intermittent setting and looks over at me. "It's good to have you home, kiddo," he says.

"It's good to be home," I say, putting my feet up on

the dash and watching beads of water shimmy across the glass. "It's so quiet here."

There are no horns blaring and nobody passing on blind curves. The road in front of us is smooth and wide, lined with hardwood forests, and the only sounds are the click-click of the turn signal, and the whistling of Dad's breath. He sighs occasionally, glances over at me, and pats my leg, looking relieved. "How was the plane trip?" he says. "Any snafus at the airport?"

"Not really," I say. "Just all the stuff I noticed from being gone so long."

At my parents' house, it is late, and my mother comes down to say hello in her nightgown. When she goes back to bed, my father follows her, and I pour myself a glass of red wine and peel off my travel clothes. I light some incense and put meditation music on the stereo. In the shower, I turn the knob up hotter and hotter. I shave my legs twice. I shave everything. Pits, bikini line. I go through two razors. Then I use apricot body wash and a loofah. I scrub my feet with a pumice stone, peeling away layer after layer of hard skin and calluses. I condition my hair over and over again, and wash my face repeatedly, until I use up all the water in the hot water heater.

Wrapping the towel around me after ten months of using my foot-wide, quick-dry camp towel makes me moan. I snuggle down inside it and pile another on top of my head, smelling the fresh laundry detergent while I slather on lotion. Then I brush my teeth and chuckle at the novelty of scooping *tap* water into my mouth with my hand, knowing it won't make me double over with stomach cramps from amoebas. Then I turn off all the lights in the house and crawl into bed without checking the covers for scorpions. The pillow smells like fabric softener, and is so soft it swallows my head.

Around me, the house creaks and I lay there in the darkness, listening to the piercing silence. There are no chickens picking through trash under the coffee trees. No dogs howling in the distance. No cats fighting. No glass breaking. No screaming. Just cicadas buzzing, and tree frogs singing. My bedroom wraps itself like a forest around me, and that night, I dream of the woods.

I wake up to late morning pouring through the skylight, and lay there listening to the sound of so much quiet. When I do wander out, Mom is already at work and she has left me a cake, decorated with sweet curvy letters that say, "Welcome Home, Cindy."

My father is happy. "The folks at church will be eager to hear about your adventure. They call you the free spirit," he says.

I don't need to tell him about what really happened in Guatemala, now that he is just glad to have his daughter back home safe. His relief is so obvious that it makes me feel guilty. He whistles all over the house and sings, *"Oh my darling, oh my darling, oh my darling Clementine, you were lost and gone forever, oh my darling Clementine."*

I try living the life I thought I wanted. I get an apartment near Philadelphia, and a job at a restaurant, and friends who like to hang out at the bar, and a cat. But two weeks after I start my new job, I come down with Hepatitis A, ending up in the hospital with yellow eyes and skin. My fever spikes at 105.7, and I am incapacitated for two months. I miss the fall, and all the dry leaves, and hiking, and the crisp air. And I blame Guatemala.

At Christmas, I go home to Baltimore, and sitting in church next to my dad just reinforces everything. The pastor goes on and on about death, and sins, and everything about the "celebration" is so morbid that I have to stop myself from rolling my eyes and making inappropriate comments. Back in Philly a few days later, I spend my 23rd birthday alone with my cat, writing. As 2002 comes to a close, I try to understand the vast scope of my time in Guatemala. But is too fresh, and impossible to comprehend. What I do know, is that Guatemala has taken something from me, and I need to find a way to replace it. This is my New Year's Resolution.

May 2003

The alarm rings at 6:00 and I open my eyes to beams of soft blue light floating through the gaps in the curtains. Through the open window I hear the buzzing of locusts, the chirping of birds, and the roar of airplanes, one after the next, flying in low overhead. When I wander out of my hotel room, clutching my coffee, the Virginia humidity settles onto my skin. I can tell by the way the clouds are already hanging heavily in the sky that it will rain before the day is out.

The rest of the archaeology crew is gathered around the vans, lacing up their work boots and sipping from thermoses, and I breathe in deeply and head towards them. The air smells like freshly cut grass, and nuzzles me into a clean state of awareness. I am so ready to get out to the field that I am jittery before the caffeine from the coffee even hits my system.

This project is an extensive Phase I archaeological survey of the woods around Dulles International Airport, for the construction of a new runway. Our job is to test all 20,000 acres of forest, digging holes every fifty meters and screening the soil, to determine whether there is anything archaeologically significant that will be destroyed when the all the trees are cut down and replaced with asphalt. The job is slated to last all season and into the winter, with a hotel room provided for us from the beginning to the very end, no moving out at all. These long-term hotel projects are the best jobs that the profession of contract archaeology has to offer. I was lucky to get hired from just sending my resume in response to an ad on a listserv called "Shovelbums".

I introduce myself to the crew, and find the man who hired me, Jim Embry, drinking hazelnut coffee, smoking a cigar, and looking at a topographic map that is sprawled across the hood of the van. "Well, hello there," he says, with a thick southern drawl. He hands me an envelope with the week's per diem allowance in cash and fishes a W-4 and an I-9 from a file box between the seats. "Just fill these out when you get a chance." He sucks on his cigar and peers at the clouds. "Guess we'd better get out there, get some holes in before it rains."

Even though it is only May, the heat at Dulles is intense, pressing down thick and heavy, like a steam bath. We are sweating from the moment we climb out of the vans and start hiking into the project area. We carry screens, shovels, tarps, and all our water and food for the day, and meander down a dirt track along the edge of a stream called Beaver Run. The water is brown and flooding over the banks, and the brush is shining with dew and alive with the hum of a million insects. Horseflies, the size of hummingbirds, dodge around our heads, and mosquitoes gnaw at our bare arms and necks.

Together, we come out of the woods into a vast area where all the trees have been slashed and left in tangled piles. Jim spaces us out along the fence at fifty meter intervals, gives us a compass heading, and tells us to dig a shovel test pit (STP) every 50 meters along that bearing until we hit an area he calls "the beaver swamp." He passes out clipboards with STP forms, and tells us to dig each hole 10 centimeters into the subsoil. We are expected to each dig thirty holes per day, and if we get them done early, we get to go home.

"How will we know when we get to the beaver swamp? Is it flagged?" someone asks.

"Oh, you'll know," he says.

Working beside me on one side are two boys from West Virginia, who call themselves Yester and Gatsky. As we work, they shouted randomly to each other, saying things like "Hoo-wee!" and "Hubba!" and "Pittsnoggle!" Yester is a college boy from Morgantown, who takes his shirt off as soon as he starts to sweat, and climbs all over the downed trees, hacking at them randomly with a machete. Gatsky is 38 and has been doing archaeology for almost 20 years all over the country, and on military bases in Guam, and in lava tubes in Hawaii. He is one of the typical, strange vagabonds who end up stuck in this profession, following the work, not really caring about anything else or ever learning another trade. The way he carries himself, he reminds me of Eeyore from Winnie the Pooh, slope-shouldered, chicken-legged, and lanky, his face sagging and expressionless. The other people on the crew call him "Lopey." Every few holes he lights a tree on fire, and Yester leaps up and down on the smoking branches howling like a monkey.

In addition to the travel, the chance to be outside every day and avoid a desk job, and the interesting nature of the work, these quirky archaeology characters are part of what draw me to this profession. They are unsettled travelers, with vehicles like Vanigans that are good for camping, and a taste for rambling, wandering, and moving on. There is a sense that only archaeologists can truly understand other archaeologists, and that we are people who don't really fit in anywhere else. Archaeology is to the professional world what San Pedro was for me in Guatemala. It is a place where I am home, and everyone else is so strange that I actually fit in.

One man, a grizzled old man with a beer belly that hangs out over his belt, introduces himself to me as "Birdman." All morning long he wanders around aimlessly, not digging any holes, just looking at the sky, saying things like "Hey, did you guys hear a loon a little while ago?" and "There's an indigo bunting around here somewhere."

Another man named Phil from West Virginia stomps around whining about the conditions, and claims to be dying from Gout and Lyme's Disease. He talks constantly to his girlfriend Denyse about being raised in the poorhouse, and being sent to the store as a child for the three staples: potato chips, cigarettes, and beer. "There's nothing quite like having your father pour beer over your cereal at breakfast when there's not enough money around for milk," he says.

A few transects down from me is woman from Maine, named Lorie. I watch with amusement as she storms angrily from hole to hole, stretching her legs out in huge paces, cursing each time she has to wrestle with the brush, slamming her screen down, and kicking the shovel so hard I think it will break. All day long she chain-smokes Marlboro Reds, and digs faster than anyone else, constantly in a panicked hurry, like she thinks she has something to prove. "When you're a woman in a man's profession," she tells me, as sweat streams down her face, "you gotta work twice as hard as the men."

At lunch, we all sit together on the bank of a wide stream near the huge beaver dam that makes the water run fast and white. Birdman tries to cross here, but falls through up to his armpits and howls while we all sit pointing and laughing at him. When he comes out of the water, he has leeches on his legs and back. The bank on the other side of the swamp is covered in nettles and briars, and dense patches of poison ivy. There is no way we will get through any of it, without tearing ourselves to pieces, so we'll have to go around.

After the rest of the crew wanders back down the transects towards the base line, Lorie pulls a joint out of her cigarette pack and passes it to me with a lighter. "I've got another one if that one doesn't get us stoned enough," she says. I like her immediately.

The apartment in Philly was an attempt to live an American life, but it didn't take long to realize that I wasn't ready for a trapped-indoor existence. Now that I am an archaeologist, at Dulles, living in the Marriott, I am transient. One day, someone calls me a hippie, and I like it. I wear the label like it is a new identity and I am starting over. I start shopping at Hudson Trail Outfitters and REI on a weekly basis. I buy raingear and quick-dry pants and long-sleeved polyester shirts with vents designed to keep the bugs away but let the air through. I buy a Camelbak backpack so that I can carry around enough water to keep me hydrated in the thick humidity. I get biodegradable toilet paper, an $80 Brunton compass, Gore-tex boots, and gators for sloshing through swampland. Before long, I am an outdoor gear junkie.

It rains for 21 days in May, and at Dulles we follow the "wet-underwear rule." If it is raining hard enough that our underwear is wet, it is time to head for the vans. This seems to happen almost every day. Lorie and I spend a lot of long afternoons at the hotel, cooking elaborate meals in our full kitchens, and most evenings we hang out by the pool, or with Gatsky, Yester, and Birdman, who act like college students in a freshman dorm, stuffing towels under the doors and passing bongs around, or drinking until they are tanked, and obnoxious enough that the hotel staff calls and tells us they are getting complaints about the noise.

One day, telling stories about my Fulbright to Lorie, I start thinking about Guatemala again for the first time since getting Hepatitis. I've blocked thoughts of my Fulbright since then, angry and hateful at the country and whole experience for stealing something from me, wanting to put the fear and helplessness behind me, and just move on. But some afternoons, when I am wandering through the woods, I almost wish I was there again, swimming in the lake, watching the moonrise over the volcanoes, feeling the *Xocomil* on my face. As the summer moves on, Guatemala sneaks into my thoughts all the time, as though the universe is trying to tell me that I left something unfinished.

Suddenly there are reminders everywhere. Every morning on the way to the airport, we stop at the 7-11 for coffee refills, snacks, and bottled water, and we wait in line behind all the Hispanic construction workers jabbering in Spanish. They always catch my eye, and start talking to me as if they know I can understand them. Just hearing

Spanish makes me ache to travel again, and morning after morning I clutch my coffee, and long to be sitting on the D'Noz balcony, gazing over the lagoon, with my hands wrapped around a mug of fresh *café con leche*.

In June, we are joined by a woman named Marina Davis, who claims to have been struck by lightning three times. She says that because of it, she can't wear watches anymore because when she puts them on, they just stop working. "It's like someone is out to get me," she says, looking up at the sky. "But I ain't going without a fight." I tell her I know the feeling. She tells us that an 18-wheeler had knocked off her motorcycle and into a six-month coma, and that when she came to, her new hair growth was stark white, making her striped, like a skunk. She is the most accident-prone person I have ever met. During her first week on our crew, she is stung in the left eye by a bee. The very next day she is bitten in the right eye by a mosquito, and now both eyes are practically swollen shut, giving her the look of a severely battered woman.

"It's a miracle that girl is still alive," says Phil one morning when we are sitting in the van at 7-11, watching a group of Mormon missionaries pass out pamphlets to all the hung over contractors. Just as Marina comes strolling through the door, Phil leans out the window, points at her, and shouts towards the Mormons, "Save her! She needs to be saved!"

She looks over her shoulder at them, and dashes to the van in a panic. "That's not funny, guys," she says, slamming the door. "Keep those people *away* from me."

Phil throws the van in reverse and peels away, slapping his knee and laughing so hard that tears trickle out of his eyes. The Mormons just stare at us, shaking their heads. Next to me, a southern belle named Heather, with a cross dangling from her neck, isn't laughing. Instead, she stares out the window with her eyes narrowed into slits and crosses her arms.

"What a fucking crock of shit!" Phil squeals between

laughs.

"Phil!" Heather barks, her loud voice startling everyone. "You can believe whatever you want, but don't make fun of other people for their beliefs!"

We all choke and swallow our laughter.

"Oh, Lord," Phil says, rolling his head and wiping his eyes. "I knew I was going to offend somebody. You can't say anything these days without somebody getting all self-righteous and pissed off." As we drive towards the airport, no one speaks, and I sit there thinking about my own religious tolerance, and feeling guilty for laughing.

That month, all five visible planets line up across the sky—Mercury, Venus, Saturn, Mars, and Jupiter—and Birdman sets up his telescope outside in the parking lot. We all stand out there together, passing around joints and drinking beer, but I can't get into the mood. It seems like I can hardly look up at the sky without feeling empty. Even though it is hot enough that we are all barefoot and sweating, the night air is cold on my skin and makes me clammy. In the pit of my stomach I am carrying around emotions that I still can't explain. I feel so desperate for something intangible, completely helpless, and utterly small. When I stare at the stars, my chest caves in, and I feel the vastness of the universe like the pit of emptiness that has become my spiritual life.

I expected to find more answers by now. But it is like I am lost in a void, being sucked into a black hole. When I look up at those planets, all I can think about is the immensity of time and space, and how nothing we ever do will ever matter in a billion years, when the earth is destroyed and life is long gone. As I leave the party and go inside, I realize that after more than a year of searching, I still have not filled up the space in my life where God used to be. All I can think now is that we are bitterly, and forever alone.

KEEPING THE FAITH

On Father's Day, Dad asks my sister and I to come to church with him, because he is delivering the sermon, and I sit in the pew with my stomach twisted up in knots. My palms are sweaty and cold, and the hair on the back of my neck is standing up on end, just like it did before the lighting struck the volcano. I don't belong in church. Just being there makes me uneasy.

The congregation mumbles through a few hymns, then a woman gets up at the pulpit, opens a bible, and reads the 23rd Psalm: *The lord is my shepherd, I shall not want. He makes me lie down in green pastures. He leads me beside still waters. He restores my soul. He leads me in right paths for his name's sake. Even though I walk through the darkest valley, I fear no evil, for you are with me. Your rod and your staff, they comfort me. You prepare a table before me in the presence of my enemies. You anoint my head with oil. My cup overflows. Surely goodness and mercy shall follow me all the days of my life. And I shall dwell in the house of the Lord my whole life long.*

When she finishes, my father gets up and says, "Today, on Father's Day, I have a story to share. Why I go to Church: Keeping the faith." His voice trembles for a moment, then steadies. "I start back on July 3, 1982. If you were to look at the calendar, you would find that that day was a Saturday." He launches into the story of his father's death from a heart attack while our family was in Chicago for our yearly visit.

I was two and a half years old, and Grandpa's last day alive was one of my first memories. I had knocked my first tooth out on his knee when we were playing in the living room, and the next morning I searched all over the house for him, wanting to play some more. I remembered Dad sitting down on the sofa, pulling me into his lap, and holding me close. "Grandpa won't be able to play today," he said. "He's gone to sleep in heaven."

They had the funeral while we were still there on our visit, and afterwards Dad spent all his time trimming hedges and fixing things, and helping Grandma around the house, trying to help her adjust to life as a widow. We took our original flight back to Baltimore two weeks later, as planned, and the next day Dad went to church.

"That morning at Catonsville United Methodist Church, the senior pastor preached. Dr. Carroll Yingling's subject that morning was the 23rd Psalm," Dad says, shifting his weight behind the pulpit. "Now Dr. Yingling knew I'd gone to Chicago for a couple weeks vacation, but he had no clue that my father had passed away while I was there. As I sat in the pew that morning, listening to Dr. Yingling's sermon, he didn't realize it, but of all the scripture in the bible, and my father knew the bible well, the 23rd Psalm was his favorite." Dad's voice wavers again, and hot tears spring into my eyes. "And as Dr. Yingling spoke about the 23rd psalm that morning, I started to recover from my recent loss."

"A few weeks later," Dad continues, "I found myself leaving Baltimore again. But this time, instead of flying, I was driving. And my destination instead of being Chicago, was a small town in Ohio, called Cheshire, along the Ohio River. My father had asked that his ashes be buried at the site in the graveyard where his mother and father were buried." Dad and his sister, Sallyann, had met in Cheshire at the only stop light in town, and found the cemetery at the top of a dirt road, at the end of a row of oak and maple trees. When they found my great-grandfather's name etched into one of the stones, they also noticed that down below was some lettering, covered in lichen and moss.

"So we got down on our hands and knees," Dad says, "and scraped away with our fingernails, and we eventually came up with five more words. Five words form the bible. 2 Timothy 4:7. I have kept the faith." He stops and looks up at the four of us sitting there in the pew. "I have kept the faith," he repeats.

My heart twists around inside me and tears spill down my face. Beside me, Sarah rolls her eyes. "You're such a baby," she says.

"Then we stood up and took in the scene around us," Dad says. "The Ohio River valley was lush and green. The sky was blue with a few passing clouds. The air felt like today, warm and moist. In the distance, we could hear scattered birdsong. And then we turned and buried my dad's ashes. We said a prayer. And then we bid each other a fond farewell."

After he left Sallyann, Dad drove back through the Ohio river towns that his father used to talk about as a boy, like Cheshire and Middleport and Pomeroy, continued across the Ohio River, entered West Virginia at Parkersburg, and worked his way through the mountains. "And all the time, there was just one thing on my mind," he says. "Over and over and over again. I asked myself that same question. Have I kept the faith? Have I kept the faith? Mile after mile after mile went by, I struggled with that question. And finally, I came to realize that I really didn't like the question very well because I really didn't like the answer. That I didn't feel I had done very well at keeping the faith."

It is all I can do to keep myself from sobbing out loud. It is impossible for me to go on lying to my dad, making him think I still believe, and I will never be able to pull it off—continuing to go to church beside him for years, pretending to pray, pretending to still mean it when I sing Hymns with my eyes closed.

"Why the *hell* are you crying?" Sarah whispers.

"Because," I say, wiping my tears with the back of my hand. "I feel bad that I don't believe in God anymore. It means so much to him."

"Cindy, you have to stop worrying so much about what Dad thinks and live your own life."

"I know," I sob, blowing my nose into a tissue Sarah pulls from her purse.

"So somewhere out there in the wilds of West Virginia," Dad is saying, "I resolved to do better. To do better at keeping the faith." He talks about turning to the church, and how much its support means. "So, in closing," he says, "I thank you for being here at my time of need. I thank you for showing me the way. I thank you for keeping the faith. Amen."

After we get back to the house, I can't pull myself together, so finally I call Dad into my room, sit him down on the bed, and say, "Dad, I need to tell you something," and everything comes spilling out in a fit of snot and tears. Walking away from my faith. The drugs. The sex. The lack of attention to my research. And I don't regret any of it necessarily. I just want to come clean to him, and for him to say he loves me anyway.

"Oh, Cindy," he says curling his arm around my shoulder. "You are always trying so hard to please everybody. You know, when I was your age, I didn't believe in God either. But eventually we all come to whatever it is we need to get us through the hard times. Your beliefs may or may not change again as you grow older, as different things happen to you. That's fine."

"Dad, I get terrified when I look up at the sky and think about how tiny and meaningless we all are—how in a billion years, none of this will matter anyway. I'm having so much trouble finding a sense of meaning in a life without God. But I know for a fact that turning back to Christianity isn't the way for me."

"Well," he pauses. "My mother used to always say, if you can make just one person's life better along the way, the journey will be worth it. She used to talk about trying to make someone smile every day. That's how we live on, in the memories of ourselves we leave behind. In the good works we do to help others."

"Dad," I am blubbering now, "in that case, with all you've done for Sarah, Alex, and me, I consider you to be a saint. None of us would have had the lives we've had if it wasn't for you and mom adopting us."

"We love you Cindy. You know that."

"I know." And I do know.

I take country roads back to Dulles that night, and as they wind through horse farms and small towns, I feel lighter and lighter with each passing mile. I watch steam rising from bales of hay, and it reminds me of the mist on Lake Atitlán. I pull over the car and watched the sunset from the top of a green, grassy hill, and as I stand there I breathe in and out deeply, trying to learn how to accept the world as it is, naked and alone in the void of space, but full of beauty and sizzling with energy and power.

As I stand there, I realized also that Sarah is right—I need to stop worrying so much about what Mom and Dad think of my personal beliefs and get on with my life. It is time to embrace the fact that I don't have to be Daddy's little girl in front of him anymore, and that it is okay to be myself. I also realize that there is nothing wrong with other people believing in God. Just because I am convinced that he doesn't exist, doesn't mean that people like my Dad, who have kept the faith, are weak-minded or ignorant. In fact, it is good that they have that support there when they need it. It just means that their truth is different from mine.

Holding on to faith to get you through the night

doesn't have to mean lying to yourself. And it isn't for everybody, but it sometimes it saves people's lives. So the question on my mind becomes this: if I know for a fact that I personally can't have faith in the God as described in the Christian bible, then what can I hold on to when things fall apart? Everyone needs faith in something.

INTO THE WOODS

On July 14, I read in the paper that the supreme court of Guatemala has overturned a 1985 constitutional ban and permitted General Efraín Rio Montt, the former military dictator responsible for the deaths of hundreds of thousands of Mayans, to run for president in the elections scheduled for November. Though I've been contemplating Guatemala a lot lately, this news hits me like a tornado, sending my thoughts swirling back there.

All day long, as I move from hole to hole, all I can think about are the people I knew and still care about in San Pedro. I want to do something to change the way things are, but I know it is ridiculous to think I could have an effect on something so huge, and I ache with such a fierce sense of helplessness that I decide to sit down and commit my Fulbright experience to paper, to salvage what I can of the Guatemala I experienced, before Rios Montt comes through and kills off everyone I interviewed, turns the lake into a war zone, and fills it with 200,000 more bodies. Over these past two years I have learned enough about Guatemalan history and heard enough stories that when I see pictures of Rios Montt's face, or even just see his name in print, I become angry. I cannot understand why we live in a world that would let him run for president after all that happened. I cannot understand how he would ever win in a fair election. After all, who would vote for a murderer?

But the corruption is so rampant in Guatemala, and who says any election there could ever be fair? After all, this is a country where members of the Supreme Court are close personal friends of Rios Montt, whose death toll is so high. And the lack of education in the remaining rural areas means that people do not know what he is, despite what he's done. People in these areas are often intimidated during elections—threatened to vote a certain way, or risk losing their life, limbs, and children. If they are pressured enough in the isolated villages where the UN observers don't go, and forced to remember how the bullet scars on their bodies were punishments for not cooperating before—if the connections and money and power aligned behind Rios Montt are strong enough—anything is possible. And if he is elected, the Guatemala I remember, that has been moving towards equality and human rights for indigenous people since the signing of the Peace Accords in 1996, will plunge back into civil war, and the cycle of oppression and poverty and genocide will continue.

And in the scant news coverage of the Guatemalan election, George W. Bush is quoted saying, "If Rios Montt is elected president of Guatemala, the United States will have to take action." I think, great. Just what Guatemala needs, U.S. intervention. And I hope that he certainly doesn't mean the kind of "action" that he's taking in Iraq, or the kind that Reagan took in Guatemala that provided CIA funding for the killing of indigenous people, torture training in the School of the Americas, and military support for Rios Montt's armies. I think of Lake Atitlán, the most beautiful lake in the world, jeopardized again by guerrilla warfare. I envision men in masks storming into villages, yanking women and children out of their homes, throwing them down on the streets and shooting them, just for being Mayan. I imagine the sound of gunfire, and of people screaming.

At first, I try to write an academic anthropological report of what I learned during my fieldwork. I write about textiles and loss of tradition, and Kayla, and the smoking Jesus, and Catarina kneeling in front of me, clapping a tortilla back and forth between her hands, teaching me. Night after night, instead of drinking and smoking with the crew, I tuck myself away at my computer. Writing fulfills me in a whole new way, challenging me mentally, and almost seeming to fill up that empty space in my heart and mind that has seemed so empty since losing God.

Then, a picture appears in the *Baltimore Sun* of the Pacaya Volcano, fiery and exploding with lava. The plates are moving, and the volcano has entered a new phase of activity. Soon, I start writing about Paul, and even though I hardly knew him, the story of his death consumes me. I can't sleep. I can't go to work without scribbling thoughts down on the back of STP forms. Slowly, this book begins to take shape.

But when the thunderstorms start in August, I become terrified of the lightning. As soon as I hear a rumble of thunder, I bolt for the vans. At night, I lie awake, with the curtains open, watching the rain drill the pavement in the parking lot, and bolts of lightning slice through the sky. The rain makes the asphalt smell sweet, rattling the windows in their panes. The shadows on the ceiling of my hotel room form a curved triangle, and flicker just like Pacaya was the night that Paul died. The volcano is still haunting me, trying to tell me that I have to go back there, that it is the only way to overcome this ridiculous and constant fear of death and hopelessness that I carry around with me, like a cross.

Living in these plush carpeted business-class rooms instead of on wooden bunks at hostels, and foam mattresses, and in hammocks on the beach, everything is different. Here at Dulles, I sleep in a king-size bed, under the comfort of blankets that I know don't have insects crawling around in them. I think about those awkward months at the University in Guatemala City, losing my faith so quickly, the majesty of those volcanoes around Lake Atitlán, and my rainy season in San Pedro, with a hundred storms like this one that made me think about death and getting high and coming home.

After we finish digging all the transects in the clear-cut, we go into the airport security unit and take three-hour tests and get fingerprinted for ID badges that allow us full access to the property inside the fence. Then we start the second phase of the project, the survey of the massive sprawl of hardwood and cedar forest that have been fenced off long enough that there are still black bear and coyotes inside, even though both are technically extinct in this part of Virginia. Lorie and I are like children out there. Completely unsupervised, we run amuck—jumping on fallen trees, climbing deer stands, poking shovels into bees nests, crawling around the wreckage of torn down houses, and collecting snake skins, turtle shells, and animal skulls.

When we leave the vans in the morning and plunge into the woods, we enter a different reality. It is our own paradise. Our secret forest that we come to know intimately. We feel like it even knows us. Before long we grow accustomed to the spider webs that hang at face level, and learn to wag sticks in front of us as we walk, and the more we get to know the landforms and the terrain, the more we learn where to dig our holes for the best chance of finding something archaeological. Lorie and I get to the point where we can say, "this looks like artifact soil," and as soon as we throw a shovel full of dirt into the screen, a projectile point or a scraper appears, and we dance around, waving it in the air.

At the end of the day we show off our artifacts around the van, where everyone handles them carefully, examining them up close and passing them around. After a while, we start finding so much stuff that it becomes less interesting, and we just chuck it into plastic bags and move on. Most of the stuff we find is lithic debitage, smooth shards of ryalite, chert, and quartz that flake off during the tool-making process.

Because most of the land inside the airport property is undeveloped, there are a lot of these little artifact scatters from Native Americans passing through during the Late Archaic period, three thousand years ago. There is also evidence of a historic town, called Willard, which was leveled when the airport was built in the 1950s. There are old logging roads, and bottle dumps with milk jugs and "Teem" bottles that date to 1952. There are ceramic and brick scatters, crumbled barns, and stone house foundations full of mice and black rat snakes.

But because I stay up so late writing, I am so tired by early afternoon that I am tripping over tree falls, and dropping my gear, and falling down hills. Most of the time I can hardly keep my eyes open through lunch. A heaviness has settled deep into my bones, so much so that it pulls me down to the ground, where I lean back against a tree and let my head droop down. Each time I shut my eyes in the woods, I fall asleep almost instantly, snuggling into the soft comfort of the leaves, moss, and soil.

As the summer sizzles away into fall, I begin to form a deep relationship with the outdoors, and I dig my quota of holes quickly, early in the morning, so that I can spend the afternoon exploring, or sitting at the base of a tree or on the bank of a stream, watching things grow. Sometimes I fall asleep there, leaning against my pack, and at the end of the day Gatsky says, "Did you have a nice nap?" It seems that I almost sleep better curled up in the woods than I do in my hotel bed at night.

October hits, and we leave the tick-infested, poison ivy cedar groves, and come into wide-open stands of old growth hickory and white oak trees, where red and gold leaves carpet the forest floor and there is so little underbrush that we can see our entire transects stretched out in front of us. These woods have a different personality than the others. They are gentle, kind, inviting, comforting like a mother. I begin to think that I am one of the luckiest people alive, to be able to get paid for wandering through the woods all day. I start to study Audubon guides to identify spiders and mushrooms. I watch finches hop around on tree branches, and hear pileated and red-bellied woodpeckers trilling and see them land on trees right above my head. I see red foxes trotting by less than ten feet away while I eat lunch. I see wild turkeys rustling through piles of leaves, and white-tailed deer standing frozen, thinking they blend in. Each time I hear the cry of a red-tailed hawk, I look up and see it circling right overhead, and it feels like a blessing from the earth. I think I really am becoming a hippie, or Wicca, or a Buddhist, or something. Without realizing it, the outdoors becomes my church.

That fall, hiking through the woods on a sunny day is better than any drug. It is where I go when I need to pray, to talk to myself, to find beauty, renewal, energy, love. To watch the trees sway in the wind is like watching a heavenly dance. To see a river raging, brown with floodwater is a surge of energy and power that can be seen and felt. To watch lightning dance through the sky is spectacular, raw, tremendous. I find ways to stay outside and to avoid air conditioning and rooms without windows. I camp. I go caving. I ride rivers. I hike. And I am so filled with the energy of the earth, that I can feel what's coming. Miraculously, everything I lost by walking away from my faith is suddenly all around me, comfort, peace, a sense of belonging. I find majesty in the woods, and in the fields, and at roadside stands where farmers sell produce, in the rivers, in the flowers, in the birds, and in the sky. And the beauty is, that no matter where I go, I am never far from my spiritual home.

Working at an airport, there are always planes flying overhead. And when we start digging right next to the runway, Lorie and I find a place where we can lie back and watch them take off and land right over our heads. I find myself constantly wondering where people are going, and part of me always wants to be up there, traveling, and going with them. I wonder if my wanderlust will ever be satisfied.

One afternoon I am sitting in Lorie's hotel room as the smoke from her cigarette curls up around her. We are transfixed by the way the sunlight cuts through the smoke, all mysterious and soft and chaotic.

"I've been thinking lately that maybe I should go back to Guatemala," I say. "The elections are coming up, and I just can't stop thinking about it."

She taps her ash into the turtle shell she uses as an ashtray, shrugs, and says, "So go."

HIGH UP ON A MOUNTAIN

November 11, 2003

The airport in Guatemala City is just the way I remember it—hot and sticky, and so crowded that I smell people's breath as they squeeze up against me to get past. I laugh to myself and think, *welcome back to Guatemala—say goodbye to your personal space.* As soon as I burst out of the airport I grab the first person I see and say, "Who won the election?"

As it turns out, no one won the majority vote. But one thing is certain: Rios Montt, who only received 19 percent of the vote, has been eliminated. There will be a run-off election at the end of December to determine the winner between Berger and Colom. Either one is better than Rios Montt, and the taxi driver who tells me is smiling from ear to ear the whole time we talk.

News of the election hadn't reached the American papers by the time I left, but reading the *Prensa Libre,* I learn that it has come and gone with a degree of mayhem. According to official reports, nine people died in the country during the election: three trampled in the chaos at the polls, and six in traffic accidents. People turned out to vote by the thousands, with long lines stretching all over the country. Once they voted their thumbs were marked with a black dot, and all the papers have pictures of Mayan women proudly holding up their thumbs for journalists' cameras. Overall there is a sense of *patria* in the air, a sense that the Guatemalan people are no longer afraid to speak their mind, or to fight for what they believe in.

In the *lancha* on the way across the lake, the captain remembers me and gives me the local price. Two little girls on the boat also recognize me, and giggle timidly in my direction. Eventually one of them hands me a newspaper, and says "Welcome back."

In San Pedro, I pick up right where I left off with the unfinished research of my Fulbright, like no time has passed. I dive into interviewing people about the elections and asking about their deepest fears, hoping to finally find some answers and finish up this Fulbright once and for all. Right away I meet Colin in a bar. He is a representative from the U.N. living in Guatemala City to monitor the elections, and now that there will be a re-vote, he has to stay longer, so he is in San Pedro for a vacation. Colin tells me that he has actually met Rios Montt, and has been in his home. The thought sends chills down my spine. But Colin also says that Rios Montt gets hate mail every day, that he is scared shitless, afraid to leave his house, and has asked the U.N. repeatedly for protection, which they refuse to give.

"Maybe now he'll know how it feels," I say, hoping it is true. At least now I know that no matter how many times they get immunity in court, no one is immune to the power of fear.

D'Noz is closed for the first few weeks of my visit because Dean has Dengue Fever. When I see him again, he is rail thin and pale, but there is a fierce determination in his eyes that I never felt during my bout with hepatitis. His expression is one of defiance and acceptance at the same time. He has accepted that the longer he lives here, the more this place will get inside him. But he is defiant in that he will never let something as silly as Dengue Fever chase him away. (The only thing that will eventually make him leave San Pedro will be Hurricane Stan two years later in 2005, and the mudslides that will bury the nearby town of Panabaj, killing 1,400 people, and causing the evacuation of the entire lake area. But he will come back, and D'Noz will reopen and continue to be the first thing tourists see when they climb onto the dock.)

With Rios Montt out of the presidential race, the mood in town is light and cheerful. Firecrackers are exploding and kites are flying. People in San Pedro are genuinely happy. Every so often a celebratory canon booms into the air, making all the tourists jump out of their skin. The air is filled with party sounds: laughter, hippies banging bongo drums, and blaring radios.

San Pedro is in a constant state of development. Throughout town, there is an atmosphere of a new beginning and a new era. New woodshops have sprung up where shacks used to be, and with all the orders for tables and chairs for new restaurants, they cannot keep up with business. The sounds of buzz saws, electric drills, and hammers pounding echo across town all day, every day. In the year that has passed since I left, the population of expats has quadrupled. There are four times as many bars, hotels, and internet cafes as there were before, and the ones that were already there have built second stories and put in rooftop gardens. For the first time, I notice that all the buildings in San Pedro are designed to be perpetually unfinished. Rebar is left sticking up out of the roofs. Piles of unused cinder blocks and bags of cement wait in storage rooms until there is enough money to build again.

I also notice that all the local men are happily teetering around drunk along with the travelers and expats. One morning just after sunrise, when I go to a *tienda* to get water, an *anciano* extends a mostly empty pint bottle of Quetzalteca towards me and asks if I want a shot. Then one day I am clomping through coffee trees, helping a friend look for a runaway cat, I stumble across a man lying passed out, face down on the ground. When I tap his shoulder, he jumps up in bleary confusion and comes after me, begging me for a cigarette, which I don't have. Up in town men are passed out and drooling all over the sidewalks like we are in Antigua or Guatemala City. When I ask Dean why, he says the harvest was good this year, and with all the new tourists, the town is swimming in money.

Everyone says hello to me as I pass. Some of them don't even know that I've been gone because they have little sense of time. Some know that I left, but they think that I was only gone a few weeks. Others rush towards me, screaming my name and throwing their arms around my neck. Even Luna, the dog, remembers me, and when she sees me, she comes bounding over and leaps up so hard that I fall down, and she licks my face like it's made of bacon. At Posada Xetawal, the hotel where I lived for so long, Pedro and Catarina have had a baby whom they named Cindy, after me. I am stunned to hear this, and realize that I didn't know how much of an impact I had made with this family. She was born just after I left last October and is already walking when I meet her. When her parents tell her to give me a hug, she totters towards me with outstretched arms, and when I scoop her up she gives me a slippery kiss on the lips.

So much has happened since I've been gone, and people are eager to fill me in. A few of the older, more drunken expats have died. There have been robberies around town by someone with a fake gun, and some large drug thefts with automatic weapons. Crank has made its way onto the drug scene, and the DEA is in town undercover, trying to put a stop to the madness. And I find out that as part of an old war vendetta, or perhaps a modern drug territory battle, a 16-year-old boy named Diego Chavajay has been hung at the lakeshore, right in the middle of the path. Whoever killed him had drowned him first, and hung him there afterwards, to send some kind of a message.

I also learn that Casa Shag is no longer rented out because of rumors that the spirit of a woman, who was buried alive during the war, haunts it. People say they have heard her dancing on the roof and screaming in the middle of the day and night. They talk about how the lakeshore used to be the edge of town, where they took people to "disappear" them, and that there are bodies buried beneath the gardens where I used to sit with Amber and Cathy, smoking joints and staring at the sky.

I am in San Pedro for three weeks before I can work up the nerve to go see Kayla. When I finally veer off the path and walk into the house, what I see stuns me. Her father, Reuben, is sitting in a chair in the center of the room, coddling Kayla in his arms, stroking her hair and feeding her from a bottle. Her hair is wet and her clothes are clean, and he tells me she has just had a bath. "Thank you for coming to see her," he says, just as he tilts his head down and kisses her forehead. "We love her so much." (*Author's note: On a future visit to San Pedro a year later, I learned that Kayla eventually got sick and died. In the end, her parents did everything they could to make her comfortable, and even carved a gravestone for her up on the hill.*)

In the dead of night, San Pedro is quieter than I remember it, with lights across the lake in Santa Cruz, San Marcos, and Sololá sparkling like stars against the black hills of the Central Highlands. And even though the wind can pick up and blow like crazy for days, the power doesn't go out as much as it used to. I like to sit outside in the darkness, with Cassiopeia to the northwest and Orion's Belt directly overhead, and soak up the silence. In the stillness, I meditate and picture the cold depths of the lake, the final resting place for so many thousands of souls, where wide mouth bass hang motionless, sleeping suspended in the darkness of the crater.

On moonless nights, the sky can look even deeper and

blacker than the lake. I find myself falling into it over and over again, marveling at how big the universe is, the complexity of it all, and the smallness of me. When the moon is big and getting full, I look up to it and see a kind face tilted in the sky, a protective force, a moon goddess. Seeing it there comforts me somehow. I cannot explain why. Perhaps it is simply because I am a woman, and the connection I feel is nature trying to knock me on the head and bring me back to earth. Perhaps it is because that same moon was there in the sky on the night I was adopted and given my name, Cynthia, which means full-moon goddess, so many years ago.

If I am still awake in the early morning, now it is because of writing, not drugs or sex, and I watch the big dipper rise in the northeast, tilted above the highland ridge as though pouring light into the sky. At sunrise the volcanoes behind me are illuminated from the top down in one slow silent motion. And then slowly, as I've seen and heard it do so many times, San Pedro comes to life.

Standing in the pasture, staring up at Pacaya's cinder cone, it is different than it has looked in my dreams. It almost seems naked without clouds around it, like it is stripped bare, allowing me to really see it in all it's towering glory for the first time. The sky behind it is shimmering blue, and as soon as I start climbing the cone, I can see the Pacific Ocean sparkling to the west, and I see south, all the way to the Volcán Izalco in El Salvador. The air is cold, and it pours into my lungs with each breath that I heave, energizing me, cleansing me, baptizing me.

Today, with my ears open, I learn about the growing tourism industry on Pacaya. I learn that the park gets between 100 and 150 visitors each day during this dry time of year, and 60-70 during the rainy season. I also learn that they no longer run afternoon trips, and that there has been one death on the volcano since Paul, a park guide who was hit by a flaming rock that spewed suddenly out of the crater. Our group is larger this time, but we have the same name (Grupo Jaguar) and again everyone is ahead of me, snaking up the cone single file. There is a couple at the front of the line named Jim and Karen from Canada, holding hands just like Paul and Lisa did, but this time I don't ache for someone to be there with me holding my hand. For once, I finally feel okay on my own, and would rather be alone on this day.

When I haul myself up those last few thigh-burning steps and reach the spot where the ground levels off, I pause for a moment, and try to remember Paul's face, and the words we spoke to each other in this spot, the last words he spoke before he died. I cannot remember exactly what he had said; only that he had no fear. For the first time in eighteen months, I can picture him clearly, smiling, with red cheeks and eyes sparkling with life.

I walk around towards the crater and feel the sharp sting of sulfur on my nose. Up ahead of me, white clouds are swirling around like a whirlpool, and being sucked down into the crater, as though the earth is reclaiming its toxic gas for a moment, and letting us see the mustard yellow and mossy green sulfur accumulations around the rim. Because Pacaya has been in a phase of higher activity for five months now, I look down into the crater for lava, but can see nothing but swirling steam disappearing into the earth.

Looking around, I recognize one of the guides, Rudolfo, as someone who helped with the search for Paul that night, and I ask him if he remembers.

"Oh yes, I remember," he says. "The Canadian."

I nod. "Thank you for helping us look that night," I say.

He shrugs. "That is my job."

"Thank you," I say, placing my hand over his. "We shouldn't have been up there in the rain like that."

"They say lightning strikes the volcano when an eruption is coming," Rudolfo says. "Maybe it was a different kind of eruption this time."

"Well, one thing that Paul's death taught me was that Nature is a powerful force, and we can never predict or control it, no matter how strong we think we are. If I learned anything that day, it is that I need to always appreciate and have faith in the earth's power."

Rudolfo nods and rests his chin in his hand. "It is true. You and I have seen what she can do with our own eyes. And if we ever forget, she will remind us again. She is very powerful, and we must always respect her."

Even though there is no lava this time, all the people around me are laughing and leaping around, remarking at the view, and at how cold and hard the wind is blowing. I watch them climbing up and down a steep ash slope towards an old crater with their expensive REI walking sticks, and feel like this moment is somewhat anti-climactic. After all the time I spent remembering Pacaya, working up the courage to come back here, suddenly it seems like there is nothing left to do but turn around and head back down, and leave the nightmares behind me.

As I step down off the summit, my feet sink in deep and the wind blows my hair back out of my face. I lunge forward, letting my weight fall to the back of my heels, gaining confidence with each step, until I am skiing down the scree slope, faster than I've ever had the faith to do on snow. Central America and the Pacific Ocean stretch out below me, and as I fly down towards more stable ground, I imagine that the country of Guatemala may be headed towards some stability too.

In the coming months, the outgoing president, Alfonso Portillo, will flee the country to Mexico under charges of corruption. Rios Montt will continue to face charges of genocide, and people like Rigobertha Menchu will continue to fight for indigenous rights. *Campesinos* will organize against a silver mine that the government tries to build in San Marcos, and they will block roads with boulders, burn buses, and create barriers with their own bodies. They will throw rocks at Guatemalan police, who will launch tear gas in retaliation, and a dozen people will die. It will become clear to the world that the Guatemalan people will not stand for oppression and exploitation any more.

Because their hostility is not against tourists, the industry will begin to boom so much that people in the States actually have an idea of where in the world Guatemala is geographically, will start to travel to Antigua to adopt Mayan babies, and will consider going there without taking a gun. I will bring my father here in January of 2004, and we will climb Pacaya together, where a new cone will have formed and red chunks of lava will spew out, and the fire inside will be red and churning like a washing machine. I will gaze with adoration at my 63-year-old father, as he sits on the edge of the crater, taking in beauty. I will tell him that I have found a new kind of faith here, that the volcano is always new, always changing. It will becomes a place in my mind that signifies the birth of all things. It is a reminder of the rawness of nature. It is the home of the earth's energy. It is a representation of the closest thing I know to God.

In 2005, hurricanes and torrential rains will bring mudslides and tragic death to the town of Panabaj on Lake Atitlán. Severe weather will continue to plague Guatemala over the years, and many of the expats who I knew during the drug days will give up on their businesses, stop trying so hard to fight dengue and yellow fever and death, and leave. San Pedro will continue to be a drug center for some time, but increasing crime will make it less of a safe-haven, and more of a stopping-over-place that the guide book says is worth seeing.

The lake itself will continue to be spectacular from Panajachel, with its three perfect volcanoes. But it will become less welcoming and hospitable as it becomes contaminated by cyanobacteria, killing many of the fish. As the years pass, the water level will rise by dozens of meters, and it will reclaim the land on which expats have built saunas, docks, retreat centers, restaurants and dream homes. A little investigation and some news articles will reveal that the lake repeatedly rises and falls by hundreds of feet in regular 50-70 year cycles, and that the stories of lost islands and sunken villages the Mayans tell are probably true. Expats will get the hint, blog about the tragedy, and call it "Paradise Lost". Scuba Divers out of Santa Cruz will visit historic Mayan towns sunken under 150 feet of water, and they will see for themselves that the lake is always changing, and has an energy that cannot be conquered.

Despite all the changes to their culture, and the shock of being thrust into the global age, the Tz'utujiil will continue to celebrate Independence day every year, and they will visit the museum to remind their children about their heritage. They will still tell stories of witches and sorcerers, and the *Xocomil* will still blow. They will tell stories of change, and of a time, not long ago, when everything was different and there were no schools, and no electricity, no internet, and no cars. And as the visitors come and go, and the waters rise and fall, the Tz'utujiil Maya of San Pedro will stay where they are, perched up high on the hill where they've always known they belong.

ABOUT THE AUTHOR

Cynthia Renwick has had an interest in Latin culture since her first Spanish lessons as a child, and the adoption of her brother and sister from El Salvador in 1984. She is a Fulbright Scholar, a frequent traveler to Central America, an anthropologist and professional contract archaeologist, a fluent Spanish speaker, and a graduate from the Goucher College MFA in Creative Nonfiction program. In addition, she currently teaches Spanish and Language Arts at a middle school in Colorado, and spends summers in Central America leading teenagers on service learning and language immersion adventure trips for Global Works. She has a husband and daughter at home, and belongs to several local bluegrass bands in which she sings and plays stand-up bass and guitar.

ACKNOWLEDGEMENTS

There are countless people who helped create this story, and it is impossible to thank them all. I could never fully express my gratitude to my family, for their endless support and unconditional love despite the truths revealed in this story. Also, thanks to my dear husband for all his patience and encouragement with this project. It could never have happened without the wit and liveliness of my dear friends Elena Cronin, Maureen Macnamara, and Jacob Wheeler, who guided me through Guatemala, and became an important part of the story. Additionally, I must extend heartfelt appreciation for the fabulous faculty of the Goucher MFA program, who helped critique, organize, construct, and guide my work. Finally, a special thanks to Lisa Jury, who was so strong on that tragic day, and, without knowing it, provided me with the inspiration to live life to the fullest, despite losing my faith.

CPSIA information can be obtained at www.ICGtesting.com
Printed in the USA
LVOW12s0148070115

421714LV00007B/320/P

ML ¹/15